THE DREAM OF ROME

By the same author

NON-FICTION
Friends, Voters, Countrymen
Lend Me Your Ears

FICTION
Seventy-Two Virgins

BORIS JOHNSON

The Dream of Rome

Harper*Press*

An Imprint of HarperCollins*Publishers*

HarperCollinsPublishers
77–85 Fulham Palace Road,
Hammersmith, London W6 8JB

www.harpercollins.co.uk

Published by HarperCollins*Publishers* 2006

1

Copyright © Boris Johnson 2006

Boris Johnson asserts the moral right to
be identified as the author of this work

A catalogue record for this book
is available from the British Library

ISBN-13 978-0-00-722441-8
ISBN-10 0-00-722441-9

Set in Minion

Printed and bound in Great Britain by Clays Ltd, St Ives plc

To Jasper Griffin, Jonathan Barnes,
Oswyn Murray and the memory of Oliver Lyne

CONTENTS

PART FOUR

What Went Wrong

PREFACE

The idea for this book came to me many years ago when I was posted to Brussels, and we used to live very near the European Commission, seat of the modern attempt to unite Europe. I used to go running fairly often round the lovely art nouveau Square Ambiorix and I mused on the curious pride modern Belgians showed in the treacherous chieftain after which it was named.

Ambiorix ruled the Eburones, and in 54 BC he rebelled against Caesar and defeated the Romans at Atuatuca Tungrorum, now the Flemish town of Tongeren. Indeed, his one brief victory over the expanding Roman Empire was commemorated all over the district. There was rue de Tongres and rue des Eburons; and I remember thinking how curious it was that here, in this epicentre of the supranational experiment, they should celebrate, in their street names, the first inklings of national resistance.

What was his beef, Ambiorix? Why didn't he and his savage proto-Belgians want the benefits of civilization? I wondered to what extent there had been Romano-scepticism in Roman Europe, just as there is Euro-scepticism in the modern EU.

I remembered the speech that Tacitus puts into the mouth of the British chieftain Calgacus, and his impassioned appeal to ancient freedoms. 'To all of us Britons slavery is a thing unknown!' he said, in words that are still echoed on the last night of the Proms.

1

Was that right? Did the Romans have to overcome violent feelings of national pride – and, if so, how did they do it? How did they make people share a common European identity – a Roman identity – when we find that so hard to achieve today?

This book is an attempt to explain how the Romans pulled off that amazing trick; and we begin with their defeat at the hands of one of the cleverest and most effective Romano-sceptics of them all.

PART ONE

The Impact of Rome

CHAPTER ONE

Apocalypse in the Forest

No one knows the exact moment when Publius Quinctilius Varus realized what a colossal idiot he had been, but when the barbarians on either side of him started uttering their war cry we must assume that the penny finally dropped. The Germanic tribesmen were in the habit of emitting a blood-curdling noise called the *baritus*, made by putting the osier-work shield to the mouth. Then you moaned down the length of the shield until the whole line of soldiers was producing a roaring noise, like a chorus of Rolf Harris didgeridoos. The overall effect was meant to be pretty scary.

If Varus was so dim as to misunderstand the significance of the *baritus*, it can't have been much longer before the first Iron Age spear whanged over the disguised embankment and skewered the first Roman legionary; and with the death gargle of that fatality in his ears it is safe to assume that Varus tried to understand the terrain in which he found himself, and to plan his counter-attack.

He was now in a place called Kalkriese, not far from the modern town of Osnabrück, today no more than a typically well-tended patch of German countryside. There are meadows and pylons, a canal and tidy little German houses. But if you look more closely you can see the same marsh to the north, the same steep hill to the south and the same 220-metre-wide tongue of land running between them.

You can also see the remains of the wall behind which the barbarians hid. You can imagine how Varus and his three legions would have advanced onto the tongue of land, marching east to west. You can imagine how the line of troops was thinned and channelled until it was perfect for ambush; and you understand how this became a killing ground, the Roman equivalent of the Khyber Pass.

It was September AD 9 – almost 2,000 years ago – and Varus was about to be responsible for the biggest military disaster in the Romans' living memory, the battle known as the Teutoburg Forest. It was a defeat that was to change the course of Roman and European history. Ever after it was to live in the minds of the Romans as a symbol of treachery and massacre, also of the big, hairy, brutal, unintelligible people who could suddenly jump screaming upon them from the dark gaps between the trees.

We have four good accounts of the battle from Roman

historians and they all make much of the trees: the height, the density, the slippery mulch of the first fallen leaves brought down by the autumn rain, the terrifying roar of the wind and the crashing of boughs in the darkness. Smart scholars these days say that this is standard Roman colour-writing about Germany, the usual tropes about the barbaric perimeter that surrounded civilization.

Yet I see no reason to doubt the broad literal accuracy of our historians. They speak of that moment when the legionaries realized that the Germans – hitherto regarded as little more than quiescent beasts, distinguished from animals only by their ability to speak – were actually attacking. It was a moment of horror.

These Romans were tough. They belonged to the seventeenth, eighteenth and nineteenth legions, bodies of men up to 6,000 strong, which had been founded by the young Octavian as much as fifty years earlier, before he became the emperor Augustus. They were trained with forced marches – 25-mile sprints that had to be accomplished in four hours, carrying packs weighing 66 pounds. They ate *buccellatum*, hardtack made of flour, and they were toughened up with swimming in freezing waters. They wore the round steel helmets with the cheek pieces that you will remember from your childhood textbooks; they had the weird *lorica segmentata*, the bands of steel around their abdomens, like some ancient trilobite. They had the short stabbing sword, or *gladius*; they had two throwing spears (depending on where in the line they stood); they had hobnailed sandals; but they had one more thing that made them into the ultimate killing machine.

The Roman legions had behind them seven centuries of a military tradition of conquest and aggression. They were the beneficiaries of the doctrine that hard training makes easy fighting, and as a nation they had an obsession with drill that makes the Prussians look sloppy. Their muscles were thickened by digging ditches and planting stockades, and devising siege engines, and throwing pontoon bridges across rivers; but the secret of their success was their ant-like cooperation, the ruthless subordination of individual heroics to the interests of the group.

By the time they came to Germany they had beaten just about everybody on the planet. The very word Rome seems to come from the Greek word meaning 'strength', and for the first few centuries after the city's foundation in 753 BC the Romans concentrated on beating up their neighbours. One by one the other peoples succumbed: the Latins, the Sabines, the Volscians, the Etruscans – all were engulfed. Then, in the second century before Christ, it was as if the operation had stepped up a gear. Whether they were being actively aggressive or dragged into local conflicts, the Romans always seemed to win. Spain was subdued; Greece was added to the Roman portfolio; the Carthaginians were finally smashed and the defeated city razed and, allegedly, sown with salt.

There had been defeats and disasters, but by the first century BC the entire Mediterranean basin was under the control of this city on the banks of the Tiber, and still it was not enough. Impelled by the lust for glory, ambitious Romans vied for military commands, and the chance to associate their names with fresh possessions.

Julius Caesar set out to conquer Gaul, what is now France, Belgium, Luxembourg, western Switzerland and a bit of Germany and Holland; and by the time he had finished it is estimated that a million people may have died. Gaul was part of the empire. Rome dominated everything on the left bank of the Rhine. But what of the right bank?

As the Romans looked over the river and into the trees, they had to make a calculation: of course there was glory to be won in those woods, but was the land worth the risk of life? There were no settlements to speak of, nothing much on which the Romans could build. There was no civilization to Romanize. The forest was scary, dark and deep. The cattle were scraggy and small. The sensible option might have been to do nothing, to consolidate the colonies on the left bank, places like modern Mainz and Cologne.

That, however, was to reckon without the Roman Empire-building mentality and the ambitions of P. Q. Varus. We have one contemporary depiction of this historic cock-up artist from a coin dating from the time when he was a governor in Africa. He has a big protuberant Roman snout, and thick boobyish lips, and a pudding-basin haircut. Perhaps my estimation is contaminated by the withering verdict of the historians, but he does not have the air of high intelligence. He seems to have been a typical Roman careerist, obsessed with his progress up the *cursus honorum*, the finely graded ladder of public offices by which Romans measured their success in life.

His father was one Sextus Varus who achieved the rank of quaestor, and then made an unpardonable political goof. Not only did he side with Pompey against Julius Caesar in the civil war of the 40's BC (in case you have forgotten, Caesar won); he then made things even worse for himself, after Caesar was assassinated in 44 BC, by backing the conspirators and murderers, conservative senators such as Brutus and Cassius. You will recall from Shakespeare that these anti-Caesareans were thrashed at Philippi in 42 BC, and the survivors killed themselves. In true Roman fashion, Sextus Varus did the same. He turned to his servant and asked to be run through with a sword; and the slave gladly obliged.

With his family history already littered with gross misjudgements, P. Q. Varus the son decided he was going to suck up, at all costs, to Caesar's heir. He seems to have been present at the Battle of Actium in 31 BC, where Octavian defeated Antony and Cleopatra. He became aedile, and then praetor, and in 13 BC he held the consulship with Tiberius, the stepson of the man once called Octavian but now known as the emperor Augustus. He married first the daughter of Agrippa, Augustus's right-hand man and son-in-law; and later he married Claudia Pulchra, the daughter of a niece of Augustus. All this is to show that he was a member of the Roman elite, and occupied a not unimportant role at the heart of the Augustan establishment. Scarred by the suicide of his father, P. Q. Varus was a toady and intimate of Augustus, the most powerful man in the world, and wherever he went he in some sense represented the will and prestige of the emperor.

He was given the governorship of Syria, and we are told (perhaps unjustly) that he left the posting having made a rich province poor and a poor man rich. In AD 7 he was given the province of Germania, and, even though he was by now fifty-three, a good age for a Roman, he decided to make the most of it.

The theory was that Germany had been conquered, largely by Tiberius brother Drusus. The theory was that Germany was at peace. Drusus had advanced as far as the Elbe, and had even been awarded the name Germanicus in honour of his achievements. It does not look as if anyone had bothered to ask the German tribes themselves whether they felt altogether beaten and colonized, but Varus decided to act on the assumption that he was the master now.

He started to issue orders to the Germans as if they were already the slaves of the Romans. He exacted money from Germany – even the Germany across the Rhine – as if it were already a tributary nation. He started to build up resentment, a resentment the Germans decided for the time being to conceal.

Varus is described as handing out laws and verdicts as if he were a praetor in the middle of a city rather than a general lost in the big wild *Wald*, surrounded by lawless tribes. Velleius Paterculus tells us how the Germans would go through a great rigmarole of pretending to be interested in this law-making, ostentatiously acknowledging the miraculous benefits of Roman civilization. They would humour Varus by dreaming up subjects for litigation, and then come ceremoniously before the Roman and ask for judgment. And all the while they would smirk and speak among themselves in the language they could not write down, and which the Romans could not understand, but which we can tell by the few words we have was unmistakably connected with modern German.

Varus ought, surely, to have had the measure of these people. He had the troops; he had vastly superior military technology, and one can understand the reasons for his self-confidence. The ancient Germans were not famed for their sophistication. According to Tacitus, who writes admiringly of them, their idea of a hard day's work was to rise late, following a night of drinking fermented barley. They would have a warm bath, and then get cracking on the next feast, which generally culminated in a fight and the amicable breaking of each other's heads. They wore trousers (barbaric gear) and put butter in their gingery hair (unlike the Romans, who swore by the efficacy of olive oil shampoo), and their general approach to life was pretty shambolic. They passed their days in sloth, says Tacitus, and disdained to earn by toil that which they could seize in warfare. They alternated, in a stereotype that has been applied to Germans down the ages, from exaggerated and possibly barley-fuelled exaltation to a state of excessive Teutonic gloom.

Their weaponry was far less impressive than that deployed by Varus' men. They had little iron and therefore few swords or lances. They had a spear called a *framea*, which doubled up as a close-quarters stabbing weapon, but many of them were armed with nothing more than missiles, and even if they could hurl these lumps of rock over prodigious distances, they scarcely compared to Roman ballistics. Very few of them had anything like the Roman cuirass, and it seems that the Conan the Barbarian-style horned helmet is, alas, a bit of wishful thinking on the part of posterity. They certainly wore skins, some of them quite snappy spotted seal skins from the North Sea, but not many of them possessed even a helmet made of leather.

What they had, by way of advantage over the Romans, was the young Arminius, only twenty-five, the leader of the Cherusci, who 'showed in his countenance and in his eyes the fire of the mind within'. It was Arminius who took Varus for a ride, both literally and metaphorically.

Arminius understood the secret feelings of the German tribesmen and the growing resentment at the way Varus was forcing the pace of Romanization. He noted the pomposity and overconfidence of the Roman general. So he decided to make himself pleasant, and useful, and to bide his time.

His most important asset was that he spoke Latin, while Varus, of course, spoke barely a word of proto-German. Why should he, when the very word 'barbarian' derived from the Greek *barbaros*, people who could only say bar-bar-bar? Arminius went along with the Roman game so far as to become an *eques*, a member of the knightly class just below senatorial rank, and by some accounts he was even educated in Rome. At the age of only twenty the Romans had charged him with a detachment of auxiliary forces, and he had fought in the Balkans. Like so many other leaders of revolutionary nationalist movements, from Gandhi to Ho Chi Minh, he was well schooled by the imperial power.

After a couple of years of Varus' execrable governorship, Arminius and his friend Segimer were so trusted by the Roman governor that they were admitted to his mess. They shared his tent; they had tiffin together and little by little they drew him further away from the Rhine and into the territory of the Cherusci, far away towards the River Weser.

'See how peaceful we are, my general,' Arminius would say to Varus (actually, I haven't a clue what exactly he said, but this, in a Thucydidean or Tacitean sense, is what he probably ought to have said). 'The tribes are happy! Rome is great, and great is your emperor Augustus! What need do you have to keep your legions on a constant war footing? Send them out to help keep order among the population, guarding the provision trains and arresting robbers.'

That is what Varus did. He placed complete confidence in his alert young interpreter and *aide*-de-*camp*. If Arminius said the place was pacified, he must be right.

And when Arminius came to him some time later, warning him of a revolt among the Chauci, he was much too trusting to smell a rat. One of Arminius' German relations, his father-in-law Segestes, even tried to warn Varus that the whole thing was a plot, and that he and his legions were in danger. Varus refused to believe it. Arminius had told him of a revolt and Arminius was an honourable man.

As far as we can tell, Varus was persuaded to march from east to west, from the land of the Cherusci to the Chauci, with his three legions and three cavalry detachments and six cohorts of auxiliaries, and one can imagine that he was in a pretty bullish mood. A revolt! That meant real military action. The beauty of

13

revolts was that they could be decisively and perhaps savagely suppressed. There might be crucifixions of the ringleaders! That meant the possibility of glory, and triumphal insignia ... and then – who knows? – a second consulship!

Varus' chest swelled – in so far as his cuirass allowed it – as he contemplated the climax to his career. 'This way, General,' said Arminius and Segimer, and for the first few miles they accompanied Varus through the glades; and then after a while they begged to be excused.

'Would it be all right,' said Arminius, 'if we went off and rounded up our own troops, so that we can be of more use when it comes to the actual fighting?'

Of course it would, said Varus; and so Arminius and Segimer went off to get their army together. While they were at it, they discreetly ordered the slaughter of the legionaries that Varus had kindly sent off to police the villages, and hastened on to prepare the ambush.

Across the whole of unconquered Germany the word was spread that a blow was to be struck for freedom, and soon a vast force of Cherusci, Marsi, Chatti and Bructeri was waiting for the Romans at Kalkriese. Even before they entered the zone of death, Varus and the Romans were having a tough time of it. The ground was tricky, and it was a terrific slog felling trees and building roads; and, like the British army that followed the Victorian catastrophist Lord Elphinstone through the Khyber Pass, the army of Varus was ill-prepared for war. Archaeologists at the Kalkriese site have found tragic remnants not just of Roman swords and daggers, javelins and helmets, hobnails and chain mail. With the help of metal detectors they have found casseroles, spoons, amphorae, jewellery, hairpins and a disc brooch, strongly suggesting that the historian Dio Cassius was right: the legionaries were not on their own but hampered by a great caravan of women and children. Because

14

some were marching faster than others, the Roman convoy was already becoming bedraggled, and then, says Dio, a violent rain and wind blew up, and they became further separated, and the ground became very slippery around the logs and roots; and just when even Varus must have been wondering whether it was all worth it, and whether on the whole he would rather be back in Rome knocking back a soothing draught of Falernian wine, just as the wagons were becoming hopelessly bogged down in the ravines, and complete disorganization had descended on the Roman army, they found themselves entering the Teutoburgiensis saltus, the narrow strip of sandy land between the bog and the hill. And then, of course, Arminius attacked.

Such was the awe in which the Romans were held that at first the Germans hurled their spears from a distance. Then they saw that the casts had been deadly, and that the Romans were in trouble, and they closed in from every side.

The Romans were massively outnumbered and suffered heavy casualties. But their training held up; and in spite of the wind and the rain and the dark, and the milling, wailing, shrieking barbarians, they managed to build a camp and to fortify it, and to burn most of their wagons. It must have been a grim night for the legions, waiting for dawn and watching the camp fires of the Germans, and one can imagine Varus gnawing his entrails in rage at the treachery of his young assistant. But they must still have reckoned that the odds were with them: Arminius may have shown cunning and duplicity, but a barbarian was still a barbarian.

The next day the Romans advanced in better order, but soon found themselves in the woods again and terribly vulnerable to the hit-and-run tactics of the Germans. For the next two days the battle continued in this fashion, with the Germans attacking in huge numbers and the Romans more or less repelling them. One imagines Varus stumbling through the ravines in a kind of daze, scarcely capable of giving orders. Imagine his paranoia as he gazed at the trembling oak leaves and the rain trickling off them. On every side he felt hostility, from a country he had regarded as pacified! Was this how they repaid him for bringing them the benefits of Roman jurisprudence?

It was the habit of the barbarians to bring their women up to the line of battle so that they could be ready to scavenge the corpses and to give encouragement. If a barbarian retreated or was beaten back, it was standard for the wives to bare their breasts in a kind of *Sun* Page Three exhortation to the troops. 'This is what you are fighting for!' they would cry, and the barbarian would pick up his sword or axe, wipe the blood from his nose, thank the girl for reminding him and run back into battle.

On the fourth day the Romans were still struggling westwards. The forts of the Rhine were hundreds of miles away, but still they hoped to make it back to safety. And then dawn broke, and with it wind and rain so fierce that they could scarcely stand up, let alone move forward.

The handles of their bows and javelins were now so wet and slippery that they could barely deploy them. Even the great square *scutum*, the embossed shield of the legionary, was so soaked that the handles twisted from their grips. Every time they tried to impose some order on the battle, and form up the infantry in a line, they found that the trees were so tightly serried that they bumped into the branches or into each other.

It paid off in these conditions if you were a barbarian, clad in nothing but the kind of fur accessories you might find in a fetish shop – a seal-skin jockstrap, a rabbit-skin loincloth. Time and again, with ever-growing audacity, the Cherusci and their colleagues leapt in on the Romans, hurled their spears or their rocks, and leapt away again, leaving the steel-girt legionaries weaving in the mud like malfunctioning robots.

By now the Romans were starting to die in droves. The great caravan of camp followers had been the first to perish, and now the odds were too much for the legionaries themselves. As the ranks of Romans thinned, the hordes of barbarians grew. Across the *Wald* opportunists were flocking to the scent of plunder and the hope of washing their spears in the blood of the final slaughter. Varus had brought with him three cohorts of auxiliaries, soldiers recruited in Germany who had taken the emperor's *sestertius* and sworn to serve Rome. Their loyalty to Rome was frail, however, and as soon as it was obvious which way things were going they turned on their bosses and butchered them.

We don't know whether Varus ever spotted Arminius, his two-faced German Iago, leading his troops in the mêlée; the young man had a reputation for being everywhere at once and it does not seem implausible. But even if history had contrived a battle-field meeting between the former messmates, Varus knew he could expect no mercy. He could see that the field was lost. He knew that he had dishonoured his name, and that of Rome. There was not the slightest chance of escape. It would be days before news of the disaster reached Roman ears, and there was no hope of reinforcements.

Varus drew his *gladius*, the sword that the Romans had originally copied, centuries earlier, from the Gauls. I imagine that he buried its handle in the mud, with the care of a place kicker lining up the ball for a conversion. He took a few paces back. Then he ran and leapt, with the determination of a Twickenham try-scorer, and skewered himself through the guts. And so perished P. Q. Varus, a man described by historians as slow in mind and body, just as his father, equally inept, had skewered himself on another battlefield before him.

At which point, we are told, all the prominent Roman officers did the same, and when news of this mass suicide reached the rest of the army it would be fair to say that morale reached a pretty low ebb. Some of them did a Varus, others just lay down in the mud and asked the Germans to finish them off. The Germans were only too delighted to oblige.

Never, says the historian Florus, was there a slaughter more cruel than that which took place there in the marshes and woods. Never were more intolerable insults inflicted by the barbarians, especially those directed against the 'legal pleaders'. That's right: they vented their special hatred on the lawyers, the experts in Roman law, the men who poor, deluded Varus believed were particularly admired and valued by the tribes.

They put out the eyes of some of these law-givers, and cut off the hands of others, and they sewed up the mouth of one of them, after first cutting out his tongue. One of the Germans held the inanimate Roman speech muscle in his hands and said triumphantly, 'At last, viper, you have ceased to hiss.'

Consider the symbolism of that insult. It was the revenge of a man who knew that he and his kind were mocked for their guttural tongue, for not 'speaking proper', for their inability to remember the blasted difference between a gerund and a gerundive. It was the revenge of the bar-bar-barbarians upon the entire supercilious sibilance of the Latin language.

Some Romans behaved badly. Latin historians award low marks to one Numonius Vala, in charge of the cavalry, who tried to scarper and was wiped out; but high marks for a classic Roman performance went to Caelius Caldus, who, on being captured by the Germans, seized a section of the chain with which he was bound and brought it down with such force on his own head that his blood and brains came gurgling forth. Velleius Paterculus thinks this showed his excellent character, which tells you something about the Roman concept of honour.

Full marks also go to the standard-bearer who knew the gig was up, but, rather than surrender the eagle of his legion, concealed it in the folds of his belt and actually buried himself alive in the marsh.

Nothing, though, could hide the disgrace of the army, the worst it had suffered since the Battle of Carrhae in 53 BC, when Crassus had been defeated by the Persians, because Varus had not only lost his own life and that of up to 30,000 men, women and children. He had lost the eagles, the sacred eagles of the seventeenth, eighteenth and nineteenth legions, the eagles on which the soldiers swore. To lose one eagle meant eternal disgrace. To lose three …

When the news reached the emperor Augustus he is said to have paced up and down in his platform-heeled sandals (he was only 5 ft 6), bashing his head against the wall. He rent his raiment, he refused for weeks to shave his beard or trim his hair, and again and again he was heard to moan the name of his dim-witted chum Varus. '*Quinctili Vare*,' he said, thudding the imperial bonce against the jamb, '*redde legiones!*' Quinctilius Varus, give me back my legions.

Varus was naturally in no position to do any such thing, but Arminius decided it would be a nice gesture to disinter him, chop his head off and send it to another chieftain called Marbod, the point presumably being to show how easy it was to beat these Romans, and to encourage Marbod to join the revolt.

Marbod disapproved, and decided to forward the head to Augustus; if you go to Rome you can still see where it ended up.

The head of Varus is allegedly buried with Augustus in his mausoleum, that huge spooky drum of brickwork, overgrown and untended and sprouting with cypresses, that looms unexpectedly out of a piazza of undistinguished fascist-era cafés.

The lost eagles; the severed heads of his friends turning up in the post – Augustus came as near to panic, after the Varus disaster, as he ever did. He feared that the barbarians would march on Rome; he put a watch on the city; he organized a recruiting drive for the army, and when men were reluctant to sign up he threatened to disfranchise and confiscate the property of every fifth man of those under thirty-five and of every tenth man over that age.

When some of the citizenry were so rude as to carry on ignoring his call to arms, he put a few of them to death. That got them going. It is reported that one Roman knight cut off the thumbs of his two sons so as to disqualify them from the army. Augustus sold him into slavery.

Over the next couple of years Augustus' stepson Tiberius and his great-nephew Germanicus were back campaigning in the German forests. But their aim was only to re-establish Roman prestige, not to conquer, and it was fully five years before they were able to reach the site of the massacre.

There is still much scholarly debate about the real scale of the *Clades Variana*, as it became known in Rome – the Varus disaster. Some say that the Roman losses were only 10,000, and that not even Varus could have been fool enough to expose three legions to that kind of danger. Others put the figure much higher, but in a sense it doesn't matter. The importance of the battle in the Teutoburg Forest was symbolic. In the Roman imagination it conjured up the idea of their irresistible military machine coming up against something darker, stronger and more primitive.

There is an *Apocalypse Now* flavour to the description of the scene that Germanicus found in AD 15:

> In the centre of the field were the whitening bones of men, as they had fled, or stood their ground, strewn everywhere or piled in heaps. Nearby lay fragments of weapons and limbs of horses, and also human heads, prominently nailed to the trunks of trees. In the adjacent groves were the barbarous altars, on which they had immolated tribunes and first-rank centurions ...

The Romans set about burying their dead; five big pits have recently been discovered at Kalkriese, the bones bearing deep cuts. But the more important scars were psychological and they were to be found throughout the Roman elite.

The Varus disaster was a turning point in world history in that after the massacre in the forest the Romans never again attempted to colonize Germany beyond the Rhine. That was it, said Augustus to Tiberius as his end approached: this far and no further. To try to conquer these thugs, he said, is like fishing with a golden hook – the prize is not worth the expense.

The frontier of the empire was established on that river, and in later years a *limes*, or boundary line of forts, was constructed between the Rhine and the Danube. We can only meditate on the vast consequences of Rome's decision to go no further. If Tiberius had truly decided to settle the land as far as the Elbe – and he might have succeeded, at a considerable price – imagine how Europe would look and feel today.

There would have been no German nation, or certainly not as its inhabitants now appear and sound. The people of Germany, like the people of Gaul and the people of Iberia, would now be speaking a Romance language. Indeed, since there would have been no Saxons, there would have been no Anglo-Saxon, and this book would be written in a very different language.

Germany would not have been divided into the Catholic and the Protestant parts; Europe, I suspect, would not have been divided into Catholic and Protestant. We would not have the great cultural fissure of the European Union, between those who cook with butter and those who use olive oil, between those who drink beer and those who drink wine. All these, I would argue, are the direct consequence of the Roman decision to treat the Varus disaster as an admonition from the gods, and to halt on the Rhine.

Above all, if the legions had gone further the Rhine would not have played its grim role in the history of our continent, the scene of hideous slaughter between the German-speakers and the French. This is not some abstract historical *jeu d'esprit*. Twice in living memory the territory on the border between France and Germany – the border the Romans established – has seen carnage that shames civilization.

It is precisely because of that carnage that we are now embarked on that great enterprise of European Union, whose avowed object, in 1957, was that France and Germany should be so indissolubly linked that they never again go to war – an objective that common sense suggests we have long since accomplished.

In many ways the European Union can be seen as the inheritor of the Roman Empire, an attempt to unite this vast and disparate territory in the way that the Romans did, to create a single market, a single currency, a political union. The difference, of course, is that this time we are not doing it by violence and bloodshed, but by the gentle lure of integration that goes with trade, enforced, where necessary, by qualified majority voting in the Council of Ministers on such details as the maximum permissible noise of our lawnmowers.

The trouble is that this project – so big and in some ways so noble – is not always popular. It is not democratic. It seems to evoke national feelings of resentment even among the French and the Dutch, both founder members of the EU, who in 2005 threw out the proposed European constitution.

Which is why we have started with Arminius, and the treachery of a man who – with his education, with his opportunities – had, you might think, everything to gain from the Roman Empire.

Arminius stands for something that the EU was called into being to solve: the spirit of nationalism, and in particular German nationalism. He stands for the incorrigible desire of people to govern themselves, or to be governed by people of their own race, or from their own language group.

For 1,500 years he was lost in the history books, and who rediscovered him? It was Martin Luther who saw the symbolic potential of the treacherous tribesman. From the Latin name Arminius he coined the German name Hermann, Hermann the German, Hermann the man who – yes, like Luther – resisted Rome, at a time when Luther was himself launching his epoch-making break with papal authority.

And when the Germans were feeling particularly glum, after Napoleon gave them a thrashing at Wagram in 1809, it was Hermann, the great original ginger-moustached incarnation of the spirit of the *Volk*, who gave them patriotic inspiration. Once again the Germans had been humiliated by an emperor; and once again Hermann stood for resistance. In 1809 Heinrich von Kleist published a play called *Die Hermannsschlacht*, which was such red-hot stuff that it was never actually performed, but became a *samizdat* text of revanchism. Between 1676 and 1910 the *Uberkraut* Hermann starred in no fewer than seventy-six operas.

But it was in 1839 that Hermannmania reached its most demented extravagance, when the foundation stone was laid for a 28-metre copper statue of the chieftain, on top of a plinth of the same height. He stands on a 400-metre wooded hill, waving his sword and glowering southwards through his moustache – south towards Rome and the threat he had seen off. By 1875, when the statue was finally completed and dedicated, Bismarck had defeated the French, and Hermann stood for the new, united Germany. It was not long before he stood for the spirit of Germany everywhere, and when the Germans of Minnesota wanted to assert their cultural heritage they caused the construction, in 1889, of their own slightly bigger 32-foot copper-sheeted colossus. In 2001 the New Ulm Hermann was voted by Congress the national symbol for all Americans of German descent.

Even today the original is a huge tourist attraction. Young and thoughtful Germans are embarrassed when you ask directions for the Hermannsdenkmal, because it is, of course, associated with nationalism, not to say Hitler: you will not be surprised to learn that Hermann was a popular fellow with the ideologues of the Third Reich.

But if you do go to the quiet town of Detmold (about 50 miles from the true site of the battle at Kalkriese), you will be interested to see you are not alone in seeking Hermann. There are hordes of young Germans playing in giant tree houses in the woods and walking the rope ladders; there are kiosks and ice-cream stalls, and a magnificent array of tat. You can buy Hermann statues, Hermann beer steins, and little hemispheres which cause it to snow on Hermann's defiant shoulders.

Finally, at the top of the hill you come on the delightfully barmy figure of the warrior himself. He has oxidized to a nice pastel green and is wearing a very tight miniskirt, and if they had featured a barbarian as well as a fireman and a Red Indian and a policeman, Hermann would have looked pretty good in the late seventies disco group Village People. In general style and concept he is similar to his contemporary, the Statue of Liberty, presented by France to America to mark the anniversary of the American Revolution; and yet how very different the message he sends. He does not celebrate a universal ideal; he is all about German-ness. He is about particularism, nationalism. The very plinth has been executed so as to belong to no conventional architectural order, since that would mean some echo of Rome. The style is self-consciously 'barbaric', with broccoli-motif capitals.

As I stood gazing up at Hermann I felt I was looking at the big question at the heart of the European experiment. We modern Europeans are divided. All the polls say so. We are divided into Euro-philes and Euro-sceptics, people who are pleased at the idea of forming a single unit out of the disparate European nations, and people who much prefer to keep to their national traditions and to maintain the primacy of national governments.

It is astonishing how closely this debate was echoed in the ancient world.

I hope it is clear from the foregoing that Arminius was what you might call a Romano-sceptic. His was a cultural, political objection, based on concepts of sovereignty and autonomy that are entirely familiar to us today. When he wants to rouse his fellow tribesmen to further revolt, he cries that it would be a disgrace if Germany were to be filled with 'axes and togas' – the symbols of domination by Rome.

And yet even in Arminius' own family there were ardent Romanophiles. His father-in-law, Segestes, was so keen on Roman rule that, as we have seen, he tried to betray the ambush plot to Varus; and a few years later Tacitus staged a symbolic encounter between Arminius and his own brother, a man called Flavus.

The Roman troops are drawn up on one side of the River Weser; on the other side are Arminius and the Cherusci. But Flavus is with the Romans! In fact, he is so loyal to the Roman cause that his face is disfigured by a scar he incurred fighting other Germans. He boasts of a neck chain, a crown and other trinkets he has earned for his loyalty. Arminius jeers at him across the Weser, and then the soldiers on either side agree to hold their fire while the two brothers slug it out verbally.

Flavus begins by speaking of the greatness of Rome, the resources of Caesar, the dreadful punishment in store for the vanquished, the ready mercy for him who surrenders, and the fact that Rome treated badly neither the wife of Arminius nor his son.

Pathetic! cries Arminius, and calls on his brother to remember the claims of his fatherland, of ancestral freedom, of the gods of the homes of Germany, of the mother who shared his prayers! In fact, says Tacitus, the whole thing got so heated that it was only the river flowing between them that prevented the two brothers from coming to blows ...

Of course there are those who say that this dialogue is nothing but a Tacitean fiction; that he is inventing thoughts and motivations for the purposes of entertainment. I am not so sure.

For 400 years after the defeat of Varus, the Romans continued to run their empire; a rule that was longer, more peaceful and more successful than any other empire in history.

The question that has always fascinated me is how they did it, and how they coped with the nations and peoples they conquered. How did the Romans create this amazing uniformity, *e pluribus unum*? What can we learn from it? And why, in the end, did it collapse?

Much of my university career was spent, alas, in dissolution of one kind or another. But much was also spent in meditation on the achievement of the little emperor Augustus, who reacted so badly to the news of the defeat of Varus.

Before we turn to him, I hope to prove to you that we are not alone in brooding on his legacy, and the legacy of Rome. Everyone has been at it.

Arminius, who incarnates the spirit of German nationalism

CHAPTER TWO

A Distant Roman Mirror

David's bombastic *Oath of the Horatii*, painted 1784: before the Revolution, the French celebrated the virtues of republican Rome ...

In October 2004 the twenty-five European leaders came to Rome for the signing ceremony. What a shindig it was.

Millions of euros were spent on diverting the traffic. TV coverage was masterminded by top cineaste Franco Zeffirelli; fashion designer Valentino created the uniforms for the twenty-five 'stewards' and female 'guides'. The Mayor of Rome flew in

30,000 cut flowers, and outside in the piazza of the Capitol – once the epicentre of the Roman state cult, the place at which all sacred processions culminated – there flew a flag bearing, in Latin, the immortal boast *'Europae Rei Publicae Status'*. The establishment of a European republic!

One by one the leaders and foreign ministers stepped forward, in the famous hall of the Horatii and the Curiatii, and signed the new European constitution into being. They took out their fountain pens and left their power squiggles on the vellum of history. Berlusconi, Schroeder, Chirac, Blair, Fischer, de Villepin, Straw: all solemnized the moment with their Montblancs.

It only remained for the people of Europe to assent to the pact that had been made in their names. Which, alas, they declined to do.

The constitution was thrown out: not by the Danes or the Brits, traditionally viewed as the poopers of the Euro-party. It was the French and the Dutch, founder members of the EU, who said no. The Treaty was placed in a state of cryogenic paralysis.

But before the electorates were so cruel as to embarrass their leaders, the Italian government had caused a marble plaque to be inscribed. They placed it on the wall in the court-yard of the palazzo. It is in perfect Augustan capitals. This is what it says:

DIE XXIX MENSIS OCTOBRIS AD MMIV IN HOC SACRATISSIMO CAPITOLINO COLLE ALMAE URBIS ORBISQUE TERRARUM ARCE IN PRAECLARA AUGUSTAQUE EXEDRA AB HORATIIS ET CURIATIIS NUNCUPATA NATIONUM IN UNIONE EUROPAEA CONIUNCTARUM SUMMI MODERATORES FOEDUS DE CIVITATIS FORMA CONSTITUENDA UT

EUROPAE GENTES IN POPULI UNIUS CORPUS
COALESCERENT UNO ANIMO UNA VOLUNTATE
UNO CONSILIO OBSIGNAVERUNT.

'On 29 October 2004 in this most sacred Capitoline Hill, which is the citadel of this bountiful city and of the entire world, in this famous and august hall named after the Horatii and the Curiatii, the high contracting parties of the nations joined in the European Union signed a treaty about the form of constitution to be adopted, so that the races of Europe might coalesce into a body of one people with one mind, one will and one government.'

One mind, one will, one government! When did the Continent last have one mind, one will, one government? Not since the fall of the Roman Empire. And it is surely no accident that the plaque echoes the old Roman slogan *plurimae gentes, unus populus* - many nations, one people.

It would be stretching things to say that the Roman empire is the sole or even the main inspiration for the modern European union; though I observe that the twelve star logo could be said to derive not just from the twelve disciples, but from the twelve Caesars of Suetonius, or indeed the twelve later emperors whose gilt-framed heads Romans would wear as a necklace.

What we can safely say is that in striving for economic and political union it sometimes seems fitting to our modern European leaders to hark back, by implication, to the achievements of Rome.

One can see why they rate Rome so highly.

Here is Edward Gibbon, writing in 1776: 'If a man were called to fix the period in the history of the world when the human race was most happy and prosperous, he would without hesitation name that which elapsed from the death of

31

Domitian to the accession of Commodus …' In other words from ad 96 to AD 180.

And here are the words of the great German historian Theodor Mommsen:

> Seldom has the government of the world been conducted for so long a term in an orderly sequence … In its sphere, which those who belonged to it were not far wrong in regarding as the world, it fostered the peace and prosperity of the many nations that were under its sway longer and more completely than any other leading power has ever done.

Rome was hugely successful, and it is an instinct common to many of us to make much of our successful ancestors. It is called snobbery. It is the good old desire to find someone in our genealogical chain who was really rather special, and to hope that by mentioning this character people will understand that we, too, are really rather special. It is an instinct that applies to institutions as much as to people, and in the last 1,500 years political institutions have fallen over themselves to claim some kind of kinship with Rome, no matter how remote, no matter how bogus.

Rome is like a distant mirror in which we try to see ourselves and confirm our inheritor status. Depending on our temperament we use the Roman mirror in different ways. Some see themselves with helmets and spears and eagles, some surrounded by saluting troops, some with conquered tribes bowing the knee, some attended by imperial good-time girls and dangling grapes towards their mouths. Throughout history, people have tried on bits of that Roman apparel to see how it fits; and sometimes it looks quite good. But no one has wholly pulled it off; neither the European Union, nor any other successor empire. No one has achieved that ideal of *unus animus, una voluntas, unum consilium*; part of our purpose is to investigate why. We must begin with the first mutating inheritor of the Roman empire, the Christian church.

The church emerged from the empire, and drew consciously on its authority. When Constantine went to the Bosporus to found his new capital in AD 330 he called it the New Rome. Constantinople has seven hills, like the city on the Tiber; but, far more important, the word Rome was an instant global designator of power.

For Constantine and other early Christians it was obvious that the pagan empire was meant to be the template, the precursor, of the new spiritual empire of Christianity. Indeed, Constantine's biographer and court theologian, Eusebius, argues that the Roman Empire was called into being to act as a kind of booster rocket for Christianity, to launch the new religion; while one may dispute the teleology of his analysis, one can see the germ of truth in the idea.

Christianity spread swiftly because the empire had already created a single political space, and because the Church mapped so easily onto the institutions of Rome. The pagan emperor Diocletian set up the 101 dioceses as units of local government, from which it was a short step to turn them into ecclesiastical divisions, each with its own bishop. Even in its pagan incarnation, Rome was already a spiritual empire and citizens were encouraged to pay homage to the cult of Rome. In the run-up to the great conversion, the chief imperial cult had become Sol Invictus (the Unconquered Sun, whose main temple was dedicated on 25 December). With a kind of monotheism already in the making, it was remarkably easy and quick, to switch this culturally unified territory to a new state religion. Rome was to be the headquarters of Christianity, not because St Peter was crucified there, or

33

because his tomb – astonishingly – has been found in the Vatican. Rome was just the obvious place to be, because the Christian Church drew strength from the name; and it was an essential part of the claims of both Romanness and Christianity that they should have no geographical limits.

'*Imperium sine fine dedi*,' says Jupiter of the Romans in the *Aeneid*: 'I have given them an empire without end …' And that was a claim the Christian Church was keen to inherit.

When Pope Gregory I wanted to underline that authority in the late sixth century, he turned back to an ancient title: he was the first to be called *Pontifex Maximus*, from which we derive the word pontiff. And who was the *Pontifex Maximus*? He was a figure from ancient Rome, of course, a politician who held the highest priestly office. In so far as Pope Benedict is now *Pontifex Maximus*, you should bear in mind that he holds a title once borne by Julius Caesar and the emperor Augustus; and the point of that name was to imbue the papal office with the majesty and dignity once associated with the emperor. And does it work, this use of the old Roman title?

Of course not: because the pontiff has long since lost any temporal authority. As we shall see, it was the magic of Rome that religion and politics were fused. In the withering words of Stalin, how many divisions has the Pope?

When Charlemagne was crowned in Rome on Christmas Day 800, he was called *Imperator Romanorum*, Emperor of the Romans, and it was the beginning of the Holy Roman Empire. It might just as well have been called the German Empire, or the Frankish Empire, but Rome was the brand name. Rome gave the thing clout. In truth, as Voltaire said, it was neither Holy, nor Roman, nor an empire, and in its Carolingian form it lasted a bare ninety years.

When the British Plantagenet monarchs wanted to assert

their dignity and independence from France, they encouraged the belief in an alternative aetiology for Britain and the British people – and one that had nothing to do with the Norman Conquest.

There began the farcical attempt to identify the word 'Britain' with one 'Brutus', who had been the great-grandson of Aeneas, the hero who escaped from Troy and founded Rome. You will find in the works of Geoffrey of Monmouth and Edmund Spenser the amazing suggestion that the etymology of 'Trinovantes', the tribe of Brits living near London, is really from Troi-Novaunt, meaning New Troy. The idea is that the British have their own special ancestry, and it's really far posher than that of the French, because here in Britain we trace ourselves back to the Trojans – like the Romans themselves! There was a time in the nineteenth century when some Scotsmen were called Aeneas, because their parents were under the illusion that it was the same name as Angus. It was bad luck on anyone christened Aeneas MacTavish, and it was hardly convincing.

If you have a national hero, the way to magnify him, to make him yet more wonderful, is to say that he is some kind of Roman. King Arthur was allegedly a Roman knight, and in chapter five of Malory's *Le Morte d'Arthur* he goes off to Rome where he is attended by all the remaining senators and cardinals and is crowned emperor of Rome. That's right: one of our key national myths is that we produced our own Roman emperor. Not a lot of people have heard that one.

All these characters, mythical or otherwise, had pretensions to be the heirs of the western Roman Empire, an empire whose fall was unquestionably a cultural and political cataclysm. In the east, of course, the Romans just went on and on. We think of them as Byzantines, but they never used the term themselves. They were Rhomaioi, Greek-speaking Romans, and not only did the empire in the east last for another thousand years, until the fall of Constantinople in 1453, but when Mehmet II finally stormed the place amid terrible slaughter, what title did he add to his list? No prizes for guessing that he wanted to be 'Emperor of Rome', and indeed the Ottoman rulers continued to bear the title until 1922, when they were abolished.

Mehmet the Turk had read his Homer and knew all about classical civilization; and yet these days you have to look harder to find concrete evidence of the Roman Empire. You might glimpse a course of old bricks at the bottom of some hole in the road in the City of London, and a Roman question mark might flash into your head. Or you might be flying over the fields at sunset and suddenly see a strange outline in the wheat, and you might think, hmmm, is this the remains of a camp? Or is it just a trick of the light?

You have to go to Bath, or Hadrian's Wall, or Fishbourne, to have a real sense of Roman Britain, and yet Rome is all around us. Or, rather, Rome is mainly beneath us. Somewhere down there in the bowels of the City there are cables that snake around the remains of Roman palaces. Tube trains plough through subterranean shrines to Mithras, and huge Victorian sewers have been driven through the ancient baths.

Rome lies beneath every major European city, and Roman remains can be found in the deserts of Africa and throughout the Middle East. Across three continents, from Portugal to Iraq, from Tunisia to Scotland, there are semi-submerged bits of Roman wall, or chunks of enigmatic Roman masonry prodding up through the pavement. People pass them without another thought, and on the face of it you might think that Rome has been forgotten, or is somehow irrelevant to modern Europe and its citizens.

On the contrary: my contention is that the *idea* of Rome is still there in the unconscious of our Western civilization. Just as the outlines of Roman street plans can be discerned across Europe, so our culture retains a deep, hard-wired imprint of the Roman Empire. It is, I believe, what Jung would call an archetype – a buried collective memory of what our continent was once like, and the astonishing achievement of the Romans in producing unity, prosperity and peace for almost 400 years.

It is not just our architecture, our political institutions or our laws that bear the stamp of Rome. We even shape historical events according to a Roman pattern, as if the Roman template added legitimacy and inevitability.

Have a look at David's painting the *Oath of the Horatii*. This enormous picture relates one of those bracing myths of early Rome that is supposed to show the unique austerity of the new power. The Horatii were three Roman brothers, and they swore an oath to go and fight three other brothers, who came from the rival city of Alba Longa. It was a nasty fight. Only one of the Horatii escaped with his life. When he came back to Rome, he found his sister blubbing, not for her two brothers but for one of the rival Curiatii, for whom she had developed feelings. Horatius promptly killed his sister. When he was arraigned for murder, he appealed to the people who let him off on the grounds that it was only reasonable to kill his sister, since she had been so un-Roman as to weep for one of the Curiatii.

This brutal tale of sororicide was painted in 1784, five years before the Revolution, and it shows a yearning for the asceticism and patriotism that French intellectuals already associated with republican Rome. Robespierre himself was called 'the Roman', and by the time Napoleon took over he was working with a culture that was already obsessed with Rome; indeed, he was working with a pre-existing historical narrative, in the sense that he, Napoleon, imitated the Roman move from republic to empire that took place under Augustus. Not only did Rome provide him with iconography; it furnished a legitimating precedent for his transition to dictatorship. Rome provided the archetype for the conflict at the heart of all succeeding politics: between republicanism and Caesarism.

Think of the political culture of imperial France: how the wily Corsican moved – like Augustus himself – from the rank of 'first consul' to emperor. Think of the eagles, the processions, the Arc de Triomphe, which is a direct echo of the triumphal arches that are to be found in Rome, or of the column in the Place Vendôme, created by melting down 1,250 cannon captured from the Austrians at the Battle of Austerlitz. What is this column but an act of homage to the great column of Trajan, with its 40 vertical metres of solid propaganda about how his troops had thrashed the Dacians, the modern Romanians – not exactly Austerlitz, but not that far away. That was the joy of being an emperor, and that was the joy of being Napoleon: you could award yourself as many column inches as you liked.

When Napoleon was crowned emperor he took a laurel spray, a wheeze he undoubtedly stole from the Caesars, and when he was painted he was painted, complete with wreath, by the same David who idealized republican virtue.

And yet how long did the French essay in Caesarism last? Twenty years. And it ended on St Helena and the emperor dying slowly from arsenic in the wallpaper.

So many people have tried that Roman style, and so many people have failed or looked idiotic. It is easy to imagine what was going through the head of Louis XIV when he had himself dressed in a cuirass and sandals and plonked on a great bronze horse in the middle of Lyons, the capital of what was once Gallia Lugdunensis. He was the man who called himself the Sun King, and who declared that all the arts, letters and sciences must come together, as in the time of Augustus, to glorify his

38

person and his reign. Louis thinks he looks like a Roman emperor; what he really looks like is a fat man in a skirt on a horse.

Suppose you are the monarch of Russia and you find yourself conquering ever larger chunks of central Asia. What do you call yourself? Caesar, of course, or Tsar, and indeed you have no hesitation in reminding everyone that Moscow has been known as 'the Third Rome' (after 1. the Italian city, and 2. Constantinople) ever since 1472 when Ivan the Great married one Sophia Palaeologus, highly unattractive and a snob by all accounts, but who happened to be the niece of the last Byzantine emperor.

You marry the niece of the last Byzantine emperor, you are an absolute monarch, and bingo – you are the heir of Caesar. Unlike the Roman Caesar, however, you are not alone.

The Serbs used the title tsar in the fourteenth century, and who can forget the Bulgarian Empire, launched by Simeon I, son of Boris? It is true that these days the culture of imperial Bulgaria is chiefly remembered for bequeathing the word 'bugger' to the English language, but by the late ninth and early tenth century they were in control of much of Greece, Bosnia and the whole of what is now Romania and Hungary. Long before the Russians used the term, Simeon proclaimed himself 'Tsar of the Bulgarians and the Greeks', a claim that was not popular in Constantinople (Rome number two). Indeed, the Bulgarians were at it even after the Russian Tsar and his family had been shot in Ekaterinburg, and Bulgarian monarchs were known as Tsar by their put-upon peasantry until 1946.

Julius Caesar no doubt had high hopes of his political immortality. But not even he can have imagined that almost 2,000 years after his assassination, in the dawn of the atomic age, he had so magnified his family name that it would still be seriously intended as a symbol of authority and respect in the Balkans.

If you are the leader of an increasingly militaristic and revanchist nineteenth-century Germany, you reach back through the mists for a national symbol and find Arminius. You build a jolly green giant in the woods. But you have it both ways. You have two superficially contradictory dreams of Rome.

You want to tap into the spirit of anti-Roman proto-nationalism – as represented by Arminius. But you also want a little bit of that glorious Roman universalism, and so without any embarrassment you also identify yourself with the man Arminius was fighting.

You call yourself the Kaiser, Caesar, a title that has been running in the Holy Roman Empire since 962, and which was picked up by the Austro-Hungarians in 1804. As the German Kaiser you join in the scramble for empire, not just because you want to compete with the Brits, but because no self-respecting Caesar could afford to be without far-flung dominions.

Even the Belgians decided to have an empire, consisting mainly of the Congo, the personal property of Leopold, and they marked the apogee of Belgian greatness with an arch of quite demented proportions at the Parc du Cinquantenaire in Brussels, far bigger than Marble Arch, and bigger than anything the Romans produced. In fact it is only rivalled in extravagance by the nineteenth-century Vittorio Emanuele monument by the modern Campidoglio in Rome, leading me tentatively to formulate a law that states big empire, small arch; small empire, big arch.

Almost everyone seems to have wanted a bit of that sexy Roman action, that style, that élan. Take the eagles. The point about an eagle is that it is the super-bird. It is streamlined and aggressive and it falls on its prey with more speed and terror than any other creature in the sky. It is the bird of Jupiter, a fitting mascot for the legions of Rome, the power ordained by the king of the gods to have unlimited rule of the earth.

That is why the bird became the symbol of Roman militarism, adopted by Marius in 104 BC as the sole finial of the standards: no more boars, wolves, horses, minotaurs – just eagles. In the fourth book of his *Odes*, Horace wants a really powerful image to describe the dispatch and invincibility with which Tiberius and Drusus – stepsons of Augustus – descended on and conquered Rhaetia and Noricum, in what is now Switzerland and Austria. They are the winged servants of the thunderbolt, he says – the eagles of Jupiter. The implication is that Augustus is an earthly Jove, and ever since the Roman Empire eagles have been a key attribute of the would-be emperors and the wannabe empires.

Charlemagne had his eagles, and so did the tsars. They had a double-headed one, facing east and west. The Kaiser had a big black eagle with a red bill. Hitler had his own specially Nazified *Adler*, and the day on which he proposed to invade Britain was, of course, code-named *Adlertag*. The modern German Bundesrepublik is sometimes almost embarrassing in its post-war guilt. But they still have that old black eagle there on the flag, if a bit stylized, and without the raking talons and the cruel beak.

Napoleon had bronze flocks of the killer birds, and he carried them on his standards across Europe in just the same way that they were carried by the glory-crazed generals of Rome. And when he was defeated at Moscow, Victor Hugo wrote a poem containing the lines:

> Il neigeait … On était vaincu par sa conquête.
> Pour la première fois l'aigle baissait la tête …

41

It was snowing and the snow had won. For the first time the eagle lowered its head ...

That was the end of Napoleon's bid for pan-European domination, of course. Victor Hugo was right. The aggressive-looking eagle was to be slowly purged from French political iconography. The Romans, on the other hand, carried them for at least half a millennium.

It takes a certain nerve to use the eagle as your political symbol, but there was plenty of chutzpah in the twentieth century. Check out Mussolini's demented bas-reliefs in his brutalist 1930s suburb of Rome called Eur. On the wall of what is now a dreary office block, we have a great sandstone-carved winding procession of Roman history, starting with Romulus and Remus, and then moving on via Augustus to mad old Musso himself, attempting a salute even more hysterically vertical than that used by the emperors. By the time we have reached the modern era, it is notable that the dictator has salvaged from ancient Rome not just the fasces – the power-symbol bundles of rods and axes carried by the lictors – but the eagles that went on the standards. Mussolini's imperial ambitions were ingloriously thwarted by Abyssinian jezails, his innings was far shorter than that of Napoleon, and after he was strung up from a meat hook in 1945 it would be fair to say that the Italians abandoned the eagle project ... with the notable exception of Lazio, the most fascist of their football clubs.

The eagle is a symbol of force and manifest destiny, and there is only one nation with the guts still to use a seriously aggressive-looking bird in its national emblem. It is no surprise that if you go to the press conferences of the most powerful man in the world, and you look at the roundel on his lectern, you will see the American bald-headed eagle, clutching the lightning bolts of Zeus/Jupiter in his claws.

That is quite fitting. America is incomparably the most powerful nation on earth, and that eagle expresses her thermonuclear ability to destroy any other nation several times over. In the eternal *translatio imperii* of history, the transfer or succession of empires, America is the new heir of Rome, and it is a cliché of political analysis that America is now as globally dominant as the Roman Empire.

There are indeed interesting parallels, not least because great powers tend to act out the Roman experience – in particular that period of the first century BC and the first century AD when the supreme poets and authors of Rome were alive, and which therefore survives most vividly in our imaginations. All of subsequent Western history has been obsessed by that time when Roman civilization made its canonical move from republic to empire.

It is a very ancient idea that there is a price to be paid for empire, not just by the conquered races, but in the ethic of the imperial country itself. The Romans modelled themselves on the Greeks, and the most splendid triumphs of Athens – the Acropolis and its masterpieces – were built not from the fruits of democracy: it was the ruthless way in which Pericles transformed the Delian League into an Athenian empire. What had been an association of democratic city-states became something else – an Athenian imperium. Great glory and riches had been gained, but something precious had been lost.

(For the pervasiveness of this motif, see *Star Wars*. I was in a state of coma, watching *The Revenge of the Sith* with my children, when I jerked awake to the announcement that the 'Republic' was being dissolved, and in the interests of security an 'Empire' was being created, with a single sovereign ruler. Someone called Padme Amidala says, 'This is how liberty dies – to the sound of thunderous applause.')

It was the Roman revolution that gave such events their

canonical form. A complicated tripartite constitution, in which government was carried out by elected members of aristocratic families, was effectively overthrown, and an emperor – Augustus – was installed. Democracy, or at least a more democratic system, gave way to dictatorship. The French went through the same process, with the same kind of fratricidal violence producing the same despairing solution: *liberté, égalité* and *fraternité* were replaced by the dictatorship of Napoleon. As we have seen, in language and iconography he explicitly referred back to that Roman revolution.

And America? Well, no one is suggesting that the American constitution has been subverted, or that the presidency is on the verge of becoming a dictatorship. But there has been a characteristically Roman transition underway for some time. The founding fathers of the United States were inspired by the tripartite constitution of the Roman republic: the Senate, the House of Representatives and the Executive. This is an echo of the Roman system, in which there was the monarchic element (the consuls), the aristocratic element (the senate) and the popular element (the assembly of the plebs). It is a trope of American political analysis that the ideals of the founding fathers are under threat.

Pundits are always morbidly pronouncing that 'the republic has become an empire', and that slogan must by now have found its way into the subtitles of dozens of portentous treatises. The Americans, of course, have nothing like the explicit imperial intentions of the Romans. There is a strong tradition of isolationism in American political thought.

And America is not nearly as preponderant as Rome. For centuries the Roman Empire produced the overwhelming bulk of the world's GDP. America produces about 25 per cent, and the proportion is steadily diminishing. The Americans have all the cares and expense that go with being the world's only policeman. Pity the greatest power on earth, hopelessly bogged down in Iraq. Does anyone else find it suggestive and awful that 2,000 years ago the original world hyperpower sustained some of her heaviest and most embarrassing defeats in Mesopotamia?

The American eagle is in danger of humiliation in the very same sands where, in 53 BC, Crassus lost 20,000 dead and 10,000 taken prisoner – and the eagles of seven legions.

The Roman Empire was to learn and recover and go on for centuries. Will America?

No one preened more enthusiastically, in that distant Roman mirror, than the British. The British imperialists were obsessed with finding, in the history of the Roman Empire, the echoes that validated their own conduct and experience.

The British didn't like eagles (too French) and went for an imperial lion; and the big cat was not wholly absent from the thought of Roman imperialists. When Horace has finished his magnificently emetic comparison between the stepsons of Augustus and the birds of Jupiter, he reaches for a new simile and comes up with a lion that is about to devour a trembling she-goat.

Lions may not have been associated with Jupiter, but they were still pretty useful symbols of supremacy. Lions ate the barbarians in the amphitheatre of ancient Rome, and in modern Britain lions are to be found not only in Trafalgar Square, but also warming the feet of Britannia, who was certainly borrowed from Rome.

At first Britannia was a symbol not of British might, but of British humiliation. She crops up in a relief from Aphrodisias in what is now Turkey, dating from about AD 60. She wears a helmet and her breasts are bare, and she is not having much fun. The relief was carved to celebrate the conquest of Britain

45

by Claudius in AD 43, and the message is that Claudius kicked Britannia's ass.

She screams and twists towards us in her agony, as the conquering Roman grasps her by the hair. Her next appearance is on a coin minted by Hadrian. This time she is seated and with a spear, but still very much down in the dumps.

She is starting to look more perky in a coin minted by Antoninus Pius (AD 138 – 161), as one might expect, since by that time Britain was a settled province. After that she more or less disappears for 1,000 years. She was revived under Charles II in 1665, when she appears on a halfpenny coin, and in 1667 she was modelled by Frances Stewart, Duchess of Richmond and mistress of the king.

In the middle of the eighteenth century people were singing 'Rule Britannia' and by the nineteenth century there had been a complete reversal. The symbol of servitude had become the symbol of world domination. Britannia ruled the waves, and the British were happily plundering the Roman record for clues as to their destiny.

In 1847 a moderately dodgy Portuguese-Jewish businessman by the name of Don David Pacifico had been living in Greece for some years when his property was attacked and vandalized. He appealed to the Greek government for compensation, and, when this was not forthcoming he appealed to the British government, on the grounds that he had been born in Gibraltar and was therefore a British citizen.

Lord Palmerston was British Foreign Secretary at the time, and became much exercised by the Don Pacifico case. He sent the Royal Navy to Greece, threatened Greek shipping and blockaded the ports for two years until Don Pacifico was compensated. It was all thoroughly cheering stuff, and was justified on the explicitly Roman doctrine of citizenship.

It was a huge thing to be a Roman citizen. It gave you rights.

You could not be subject to arbitrary chastisement. When the apostle Paul is about to be flogged in Jerusalem, he turns to the centurion and plays his get-out-of-jail card. 'I am a Roman citizen,' he says. And the centurion goes to the chief captain, and says, ''Ere, Sarge, this fellow says he is a Roman citizen.' And then the chief captain comes to Paul, and says, 'Is that so?' Are you a Roman? And Paul says 'Yes,' and that's enough. The flogging is abandoned.

Such was the terror of the name of Rome. Paul was a Jew from Tarsus, but he had Roman citizenship, and it was Palmerston's objective to show that Britain was the new Rome, and that no matter how remote he might be – a Portuguese Jew like Don Pacifico living in Greece – a British citizen was still a British citizen, and entitled to the full protection of the gunboats.

Everywhere you looked in the British Empire there were little evocations of Roman precedent. People were sent out as 'proconsuls'. Disraeli produced the pompous but essentially bogus slogan '*imperium et libertas*' – empire and liberty. Before the First World War, Lord Cromer, the colonial administrator Evelyn Baring, wrote a strange and suggestive essay called 'Imperialism Ancient and Modern', in which he used the Roman example to mount a justification for the British possession and retention of India.

It is 1909 and Cromer, a highly intelligent man and no mean classicist, is struggling with the morality of hanging on to the Indian colony. What are we doing? he asks himself. Where are you going, Britannia? *Quo vadis*, eh? He wonders what the ancient Roman imperialist would have considered his duty, and concludes that it would have been at all costs to maintain the empire, to civi-lize and Romanize the people within it, and to preserve good governance.

The objectives of the British imperialist, he concludes,

must be roughly the same. India is so diverse, with 147 different languages, and the Hindoos so at odds with the Mohammedans, and so forth, that it would not only be wrong for Britain to abandon the jewel in her imperial crown. 'It would be a crime against civilization.'

> It may be that at some future and far distant time we shall be justified in handing over the torch of progress and civilization in India to those whom we have ourselves civilized. All that can be said at present is that until human nature entirely changes, and until the racial and religious passions disappear from the face of the earth, the relinquishment of that torch would almost certainly lead to its extinction.

Well, the truth is he was partly justified in his foreboding. The birth of modern India, which took place forty years after his warning, was certainly bloody, and the tension between India and Pakistan is still talked of as one of the greatest potential threats to world peace.

As he considers the future problems of post-British India, the lugubrious, cockaded old Cromer has a further and more profound insight – an insight on which I hope to expand and place at the heart of this book.

The British liked to bang on about their Roman pretensions, and Cromer is no exception. He notes the similarities in the way the empires were formed, with young thrusters heading out for glory, and the news of their conquests greeted with some dismay by the elite of the metropolis. Warren Hastings had his counterparts in ancient Rome, and his counterparts also had their enemies. Like the British, the Romans had a moral ambivalence about what they were doing.

Some of the aristocracy were actively hostile to the acquisition of new territories, thinking that all this loot was bad for the

soul, and that expansion would inevitably bring in strange un-
Roman beliefs and practices, and that it would end up with a
weakening of their civilization.

The elder Cato was always moaning about the loss of the
old republican virtues, and has been called a 'little Roman', on
the model of 'Little Englander'. In just the same way, the arch-
anti-imperialist J. A. Hobson wrote a marvellous rant against
empire in 1902 – to which Cromer's work may be seen as a
kind of response:

> A nation may either, following the example of Denmark or
> Switzerland, put brains into agriculture, develop a finely varied
> system of public education, general and technical, apply the
> ripest science to its special manufacturing industries, and so
> support in progressive comfort and character a considerable
> population upon a strictly limited area; or it may, like Great
> Britain, neglect its agriculture, allowing its land to go out of
> cultivation and its population to grow up in towns, fall behind
> other nations in its methods of education and in the capacity of
> adapting to its uses the latest scientific knowledge, in order that
> it may squander its pecuniary and military resources in forcing
> bad markets and finding speculative fields of investment in
> distant corners of the earth, adding millions of square miles
> and unassimilable population to the area of the empire.

Thus Hobson at the beginning of the last century. Vaguely
similar sentiments can be found in Roman authors such as
Florus, writing in the age of Hadrian and Trajan, who says it
might have been better if Rome had been content with the
provinces of Sicily and Africa, rather than that she should grow
to such strength as to be ruined by her own greatness.

All these, says Cromer, are points of comparison between
the British and the Romans, races united in their tendency to

moral debate, to a certain practicality, to martial qualities and the way their characters both 'appear to best advantage in critical times'.

But there is one huge difference between British and Roman imperialism, and it prompts Cromer to his gloomiest meditations. The trouble with us British, he says, is that we are just not as skilled as the Romans at assimilating the conquered territories. This was the supreme genius of the Roman imperial technique. They 'either Romanized the races who were at first their subjects and eventually their masters, or left those races to be the willing agents of their own Romanization'.

And us? Well, the trouble is that we are a bit stuffy, says old Cromer. 'Our habits are insular,' says the earl, 'and our social customs render us, in comparison at all events with the Latin races, somewhat unduly exclusive. These are characteristics which tend to create a barrier between the British and the more educated portion of the subject races.'

Cromer is honest about the problem in a way that few have been able to be honest in the last fifty years. The problem, bluntly, is partly that we are snobbish and racist, he says, and so there has been no proper 'fusion' between the British and their alien subjects.

But then there is a further and deeper problem, and one the Romans did not have to face until the end of their empire. For centuries the Romans conquered tribes whose religion presented no real barrier to assimilation. The Romans were both cunning and easy-going. As we shall see, they welcomed new gods and just merged local gods with Roman divinities. Lug became Mercury, the Syrian god Bel was transformed into Jupiter Belos, and so on.

But when the Romans came up against the two great militant and proselytizing faiths – Christianity, and its offshoot, Islam – the limits of assimilation were reached.

50

There could be no compromise, no possibility of happy co-existence, with these faiths that insisted on the unique truth of their own creeds. In the end, Rome was to be conquered by Christianity, and much of the Roman Empire – above all the North African breadbasket and the eastern Mediterranean – was eventually to fall to Islam.

By the time the British came to conquer India and other parts of Asia, the old Roman approach – of assimilation and happy miscegenation – had been abandoned. Perhaps the single biggest and most important difference between the Roman and the British empires is in the gift of citizenship, made universal throughout the Roman world in AD 212. The British could not have dreamt of any comparable enfranchisement.

In the Roman world, anyone was a potential Roman citizen. The British thought their subjects too many and too strange.

The British approach was essentially communalistic: that is, to acknowledge the insurmountable barriers between the faith groups and to allow them to live in their own structures and with their own hierarchies. They did their best to ban some of the more revolting practices, such as suttee, but not because they particularly wanted to assert their authority over the religion. They just thought it was a bit off for a widow to be bullied into burning herself alive.

It was very different with the Romans. When they banned the Gaulish druids from performing human sacrifice, there was no particular moral sensitivity at stake. They just didn't like anyone else having the power of life and death.

As Cromer acknowledges, the Romans assimilated successfully and created a universal sense of Romanness; and for reasons of racism, religion and cultural prejudice on both sides, the British have failed to create anything like a comparable sense of Britishness, either abroad or, indeed, at home. Now we are dealing with the consequences, in Britain, of adopting that communalistic approach, as the children of our imperial possessions grow up, in our own cities, in a way that is often balkanized and alienated. It was that Roman genius for assimilation – making people want to be Roman – that did the trick for so many centuries.

And that, really, is why Rome has been so heavily imitated. It wasn't just the militarism, or the uniforms, the salutes, the hint of orgies. It was the sheer economic success and peacefulness of this rich and varied monoculture.

It is that memory, of a peaceful and united continent, that is so appealing. It tolls to us across the ages, like the church bell of a sea-drowned village. It is a like a memory of childhood bliss that the elderly continent has struggled ever after to recapture. That success is what the great European tyrants and dictators have tried to recreate; and that, of course, is why the latest and most ingenious attempt to rebuild the Roman Empire – and create a single harmonious economic and political union – should have begun in the Eternal City.

It is a formidable ambition, and one would have to be a pretty hard-bitten sort of Euro-sceptic not to be filled with admiration for what they are trying to achieve. Call me idealistic, but I think it would be a rather wonderful thing if the peoples of Europe did indeed share the same mind and will. Believe me, they do not, nor are they likely to do so in my lifetime or yours.

In AD 417 the pagan poet Rutilius Namatianus wrote in praise of Rome a poem that is all the more poignant considering that the ravages of the barbarians had already begun. 'You have made out of diverse races one *patria*, one country,' he said. 'You have made a city out of what was the world.'

The Romans did indeed achieve the creation of a European

patria. It is time now to consider how they did it, how they produced that magical process of assimilation.

We begin with the man who was so instrumental in setting up the Roman imperial system that he has been called the godfather of Europe: the emperor Augustus.

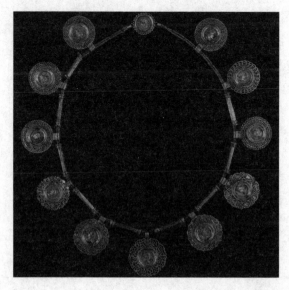

The emperor necklace – uncannily like the euro flag

PART TWO

At the Centre of the Web

CHAPTER THREE

A Master of Propaganda

Augustus in military dress
The man who made it all possible

Apart from the current ruler of Turkmenistan, whose bizarre reforms seem unlikely to endure, only two human beings have given their names to the months of the year, and one was the adoptive son of the other. Their names have come down into common speech, into every diary and every form of daily record in the West and beyond.

That's what I call a legacy. These two brutal dictators have baulked so huge in the imagination of Europe that they have survived every ecclesiastical reform of the calendar, even though they were both pagans.

We celebrate Christmas for – what? – two days of the year. We mark the nativity of our Saviour with a brief, cold interval of wassail, acrimony and guilt.

The serious holidays begin with July, the month that was named in honour of Gaius Julius Caesar in 44 BC, the year he was assassinated. But it is during the month that was named after Augustus that Western civilization celebrates with the greatest expenditure and the most ferocious relaxation.

From Washington to Moscow, from Berlin to Brussels, the official classes head for the hills and the beaches, and in 1,000 years the name of the Roman tyrant will still sound in our ears with the suggestion of leisure and fun. And I would say that is no accident.

There is a deep logic in the decision to preserve the names of Julius and Augustus Caesar. It reflects their pivotal role in the creation of our European civilization.

The senate's decision to rename the fifth month (as it was) in honour of Julius was ostensibly to thank him for sorting out the calendar, which had fallen into disrepute. The office of *Pontifex Maximus*, the priest who was responsible for deciding when the year ended, had become corrupt. Roman officials were being extended in their offices by adding days to the year, to the point where January had started to fall in the autumn.

Julius Caesar fixed that, bringing the seasons back in harmony with the calendar, in a cosmic demonstration of his power. The name of the month was supposed to be a thank-you present; in reality, it reflected the desire of the senate to suck up to the dictator, a man who had not hesitated to lead his troops on Rome.

Fifteen years later the Roman senate decided to name the sixth month (as was) in honour of Augustus, and a victory in battle. The Roman historian Dio Cassius does not normally give us dates of battles, but he believed Actium deserved to be remembered. He was surely right. It was on 2 September 31 BC that Augustus took sole charge of Rome. It was the beginning of a new world order.

Not so very long ago my family and I arrived at the Greek airport of Preveza, rather late at night, to find that I had made a cock-up. The hire car was too small for our needs, and, as I stood in despair looking at the map and pondering bus routes, I noticed that the name of the airport was in fact Preveza-Aktio.

'Hey,' I said to my wife, 'guess what! It's Actium! All my life I have wanted to see Actium.'

'Yeah,' she said in the tones of one still waiting for the right hire car to show up. 'And some of us want to see some action from you.'

'No, no,' I said. 'I mean *Actium*, the hinge of fate, the turning point of human destiny.' And over the next few days I tried to explain the importance of this battle.

On the last day, as we went back to the airport, we made a special detour, past the Ambracian Gulf, with its salt flats and pelicans, and out to the promontory of Actium, one of two crab-like pincers of land at the mouth of the gulf.

It must have been here, I said to my family – who heroically feigned interest – that Antony had his tents. You know Antony, the guy who loved Cleopatra.

As we looked out over the winking sea, as blue as corn-flowers, I am afraid I was suddenly overcome with a burst of schoolmasterly zeal. I could imagine how it must all have been.

Here on this promontory were Antony and Cleopatra, and somewhere close to where we were standing was the camp in which they spent the night before the battle – the *conopia*, the mosquito nets with their Graecizing names, redolent of luxury – that are mentioned by the ancient poets. Here the couple did some last-minute Burton–Taylor smooching before embarking on their vessels, Cleopatra to her squadron of sixty ships, Antony to a little dinghy in which he was rowed round his 500-strong navy to give encouragement. Some of his ships were huge, like triremes but with ten banks of oars – dekaremes. They loomed out of the water, says Virgil, like the Cycladic islands.

Over the water on the northern promontory – only a few hundred yards away – was Gaius Julius Caesar Octavianus. He also had a powerful navy stationed in the gulf – though his ships lacked the gigantism of Antony's. With only 400 on the water, he also lacked the numbers.

The stakes could not have been higher. Antony's game was to smash out through the crab pincers and, eventually, take the fight to Italy. Octavian's objective was to keep him there and crush him.

Now, if you looked at the military form of the two men you might have predicted a win for Antony. His vigour was famous. He had fought a gruelling campaign against the Parthians – Rome's most dangerous foe – and not entirely without distinction. He was loved by his troops and his friends alike. In his character and physical strength he was likened to Hercules, and even wore a Herculean lion skin over his shoulders.

Octavian, on the other hand, was small, pale and sickly. He had no particular record of physical bravery or military skill, and, though he had been involved in several highly successful campaigns, the real work always seemed to be done by other generals.

But if you thought more deeply about the character behind that fine-boned, smooth-skinned face, there were clear signs that Octavian was the cornflake that gets to the top of the packet. The great lovers were doomed.

Octavian had done well even to become the heir of Caesar. He was only a great-nephew, and there were two other great-nephews who were older than him, both with a marginally better claim to preferment. But Caesar seems to have spotted something in the kid.

The two probably met when Caesar returned from his battles with Pompey in 47 BC and immediately had the sixteen-year-old elected to the college of pontifices. Then he asked him to come on his next campaign, against the Pompeians in Africa. One can imagine how exciting it must have been for Octavian to receive this favour from the conqueror of Gaul and Britain. But Octavian's mother, Atia, said her boy was too young and vetoed the proposal; and so Caesar consoled him, on his return from thrashing Pompey, by giving him military decorations and allowing him to march in his triumph. He raised his young, slightly less well-born kinsman to the patricians – the aristocracy – and allowed him to preside over some lavish games.

For a seventeen-year-old it was all a bit much. Octavian fell ill, and when Caesar marched off again, this time to beat up the sons of Pompey, Octavian was too weak to follow.

Never mind, said Caesar. You just get well and follow when you can. So he did. He travelled under his own steam, surviving a shipwreck and so impressed Caesar by his pluck that the dictator took Octavian on his staff for projected fresh campaigns against the Parthians, in the east, and against the Dacians north of the Danube. But before Octavian could prove himself further, Caesar decided that he should complete his education in the Greek city of Apollonia, in what is now Albania. He was studying there with his friend Marcus Vipsanius Agrippa when terrible news reached him from Rome.

Rome was built on the desire of aristocrats to obtain glory. Glory was obtained by military victory. Military victory was obtained by deploying an army better disciplined and more aggressive than anything the world had known.

For seven centuries Rome had been steadily expanding. She took out the neighbouring towns, and still the hunger for conquest was not satisfied. Sometimes the old guard disapproved of this egotistical glory-mania, and sometimes Rome was dragged into conflicts she did not start. But she always seemed to come out on top.

North Africa, Greece and Spain were added to the Roman Empire – long before the Romans had an emperor – and no power seemed able to resist them. It was as if some new predator had entered the ecosystem, with no equal in ferocity. It was inevitable that the very instrument of Roman success would eventually be turned on the Romans themselves. The army and the generals became impossible to control.

Like everything the Romans did, their politics were highly competitive, and after the expulsion of the kings in 509 BC they were governed by an elaborate quasi-democracy in which aristocrats vied for public office. But it was a frail kind of democracy and vulnerable to men with stout hearts and sharp swords. For most of the first century before Christ the Roman world was beset by civil wars, as one general after another was seized by that sudden nostril-flaring realization that the state was in danger – and he was the man to save it. Sulla fought Marius, and then invested the city with his own troops. He launched terrible purges of his enemies – called Proscriptions –

in which the names of the victims were posted in the Forum. Then Caesar and Pompey fell out, and in 49 BC Caesar decided he was above the law. He crossed the Rubicon at the head of his own troops – an act forbidden to generals – and, like Sulla, marched on Rome.

He became a dictator and, by definition, a blot on the constitution. The pretence of democracy was becoming painfully thin. The old-fashioned conservatives and republicans were becoming more and more unhappy.

Caesar was as blue-blooded as they come, but other aristocrats resented him for his flashy populism. He was suspected of wanting to be a king. Among those with deep doubts were Cicero, the orator, whose political skills never quite matched his literary genius, and noblemen like Brutus and Cassius.

On 15 March 44 BC Caesar attended the senate in Pompey's great hall, laughing off both the bad dreams of his wife and the warnings of a soothsayer. At first he did not understand the intentions of a crowd of about sixty senators who pressed about him with petitions, forcing him down with their kisses into his gilded chair. Then he felt his toga being pulled down, to expose his breast. 'But this is violence!' he is reported to have complained. Then Casca struck the first blow. Again and again the dictator was stabbed, from the chest to the groin. Seeing that one of his assailants was Brutus, whose mother Servilia he had loved in his youth, he said, 'You, too, my child.'

Not wishing to be seen in his death agony, he furled his toga over his face and fell at the base of Pompey's statue.

It was now that Octavian began to show the courage and cunning that must rank him among the most brilliant politicians of history. If you wanted to create a First XI of history's world-class statesmen, you'd pick Augustus as your midfield playmaker.

(It is a mark of his protean political talents that our hero keeps changing his name. Before the death of Julius Caesar he is known as Gaius Octavius; thereafter he becomes Gaius Julius Caesar Octavianus; and after he becomes emperor in 27 BC he is known as Caesar Augustus, or Augustus Caesar, or just Caesar, or just Augustus. Got it? Let's call him Octavian until Actium, and Augustus thereafter.)

One can imagine his feelings on hearing that his revered and admired great-uncle had been murdered. There was rage at the loss of a relative, rage against his killers and rage that his path to advancement had been suddenly cut off. But he acted with immense coolness and care.

In Rome all eyes were on Mark Antony, who shared the consulship with Caesar and who had made a histrionic speech over the corpse of the dictator, whipping up the crowd into an ecstasy of revenge. Octavian was a distant relation, both geographically and in his bloodlines. He was only eighteen.

But, as he discovered when he arrived in Italy, he had a huge advantage over everyone else. He had been named in Caesar's will as his heir.

Don't do it, his stepfather Philippus urged him. Don't take up the inheritance. Be good to yourself, my boy. Have a quiet life. The young man ignored him.

He marched to Rome, and as he progressed the veterans of Caesar's campaigns flocked to his banner. He went to see Mark Antony, to claim the huge Caesarian fortune that was his due. Now Antony made his first mistake. He treated the young man rudely. Sorry, he said, the money's gone (the truth is that Antony had spent it). Octavian was denied about 100 million sesterces, money that Caesar had intended for the urban poor of Rome and for his troops.

A less intelligent man might have decided there and then to become a sworn enemy of Antony. Octavian could have made a tactical alliance with the anti-Caesarian faction, the men who had killed his great-uncle. He could have joined the war on Antony in the hope of installing himself as the new power in Rome. Cicero was among those who urged him to do just that. Octavian was much too fly to agree.

If he aligned himself with Cicero and the opponents of Antony, he would be making common cause with Brutus and Cassius, the men who had killed his adoptive father. That prospect he may well have found disgusting. But he had shrewder reasons for biding his time.

The trouble with Cicero was that, for all his rhetorical brilliance, he was a second-rate politician. He expended torrents of verbiage burnishing the memory of his own consul-ship in 63 BC when he had heroically thwarted the somewhat nebulous Catiline 'conspiracy' against the state. He bored for Rome about the importance of the old way of doing things; he loathed the militarism and opportunism of Caesar. He was fundamentally right, but always let down by his own vanity and self-importance.

He saw himself as the inveterate protector of the republic; he hailed the assassination on the Ides of March as a 'liberation' and spoke of Brutus and Cassius as liberators. What did he see in Octavian? No more than a useful agent for the destruction of Antony and the extermination of Caesarism. He did not trust Octavian. Of course not. But, then, he did not think Octavian would matter much in the long run, and he produced one of those little quips of which he was so fond and which was to cost him his life. He let fall that the young man was *laudandum, ornandum, tollendum*. He was to be praised, honoured, extolled – except that *tollendum* could also mean 'to be removed'. It was quite droll, but it wasn't clever, and it came to the ears of Octavian.

Again the young man was too cool to take instant offence.

The gag merely confirmed his analysis that there was no case for going over entirely to the anti-Caesarian gang. Apart from anything else, Brutus and Cassius were lined up to take over as consuls in the next couple of years, and there was no room for him in the timetable.

So he played both ends off against the middle. He was involved in actions against Antony in April 43 BC, but somehow refused to follow them up. When the republicans came to see him, and begged him to help them chase Antony down, he said that his troops – many of whom had been loyal to Caesar – would not obey the order.

Octavian had worked out that his best bet was first to destroy the killers of Caesar, and then to take over the Caesarian faction. Of course Antony would ultimately find himself in the way. But first things first.

Early in June 43 BC Cicero wrote proudly to Brutus, the conspirator, that he had scotched any plans Octavian might have had to ascend to the consulship. On 27 June he sent another letter to Brutus, who had by now taken charge of large areas of northern Greece. Things still looking good on the Octavian front, boasted Cicero. He's gonna be pliable. Oh yes: I am pretty sure I can persuade the lad to give up his ambition.

It can have been only a few days later that Octavian sent a deputation of 400 centurions to the senate requesting that their commander be made consul. 'If you do not make him consul,' said the leading member of the delegation, drawing his sword, 'this will!' The senate panicked. They tried a brief resistance, but the legions in Rome went over to Caesar's heir.

A few days later, Octavian was made consul in succession to his adoptive father Julius. It was an astonishing and outrageous coup, not least because he was only twenty and therefore twenty-two years younger than the legal minimum for holding that office.

We must now spool forward quickly through twelve hectic and violent years. Somehow or other the two principal combatants of Actium – Octavian and Antony – contrived to remain in an alliance. In the long run, though, they were on a collision course, for several reasons.

There was the overwhelming ambition of Octavian, and his almost supernatural will to power. There was the risk that Antony would set up a rival imperium in the east, possibly based in Alexandria. In the end, though, we must acknowledge the romantic school of history. It was ultimately a woman who came between them.

In 43 BC, the year Octavian became consul, the two men did the smart thing. Together with Lepidus, a man of lesser energies, they met at a river island near Bononia, modern Bologna. They did a deal. They agreed that they would form a triumvirate, a three-man commission for the salvation of the Roman republic. They then set about their enemies.

First they launched their own proscriptions, the ruthless acts of extra-judicial murder they had learned from Sulla. You remember the scene from Shakespeare ('Look, with a spot I damn him') and the horrible heartlessness with which the death list was drawn up. Antony's top target was Cicero. The old boy had persecuted Antony with his Philippics, laying into his character and sex life with a style that was scabrous even by the standards of Roman invective. Octavian did nothing to protect him. *Laudandum, ornandum, tollendum*, Cicero had said of Octavian, and thought it a good crack. Well, now the joke was on Cicero.

The old man fled to the coast and was making a half-hearted attempt to escape in his litter when he was overtaken by a centurion on 7 December 43 BC. He put down his copy of Euripides' *Medea* and stuck his head out of the window. 'Here, veteran,' he said, offering his throat, 'if you think it right, strike.' The centurion took his head off in three blows.

Afterwards some claimed that Octavian had wrangled for two days with Antony and tried to keep Cicero off the list. There seems no reason to believe it. For Octavian, what mattered was expediency. It was, for the present, expedient to be on the side of Antony.

At Philippi in Macedonia, in 42 BC, they together fought one of the decisive battles of the Western world. The Caesarians met the anti-Caesarians. There were twenty legions on each side, and by the end Brutus, Cassius and the republican cause were all dead amid pitiable scenes of bungling, suicide and bungled suicide. Once again Octavian fell ill and played little part in either of the two big encounters. Antony took most of the military credit. But it was still a joint operation.

Hopes for this Antony–Octavian alliance rose still further in 40 BC, when Antony married Octavia, the sister of Octavian. What could more perfectly symbolize the new attachment between the two rivals? They were family, weren't they? But if a dynastic marriage is capable of sweetening the dynasts, a broken dynastic marriage is poison.

The broad terms of the triumvirate were that Octavian would manage Italy and the western empire, while Antony would control the ineffable riches of the east. Lepidus was to get Africa, the wooden spoon.

It was the previous year in Cilicia, on a river in what is now southern Turkey, that Antony had met the woman who was to bewitch him and to be his downfall. She was twenty-eight and Plutarch says she was at the very peak of her beauty, and, though she had not a drop of Egyptian blood in her veins, she was the queen of Egypt.

Seven years before she first met Antony, Cleopatra had already won the heart of Julius Caesar, famously arriving in his presence in a bolt of cloth or carpet, which was unrolled before him. She used that alliance not only to produce an heir – Caesarion – but also to turn Caesar's troops on her enemies and to secure her position as Pharaoh.

Now she set about the seduction of Antony with brilliant professionalism. Plutarch has given us a breathtaking account of her appearance on the golden poop of her barge, its purple sails billowing in the wind, while her rowers caressed the water with oars of silver which dipped in time to the music of the flute. Cleopatra herself was dressed as Venus, reclining beneath a canopy of cloth of gold, and on either side of her couch were boys dressed as Cupid cooling her with their fans.

Antony had summoned her to his presence because she was suspected of supporting Cassius in the recent conflict, and he wanted an explanation. It seems unlikely that he got one.

Plato says that there are four kinds of flattery. Plutarch says that she possessed a thousand: above all, the mimetic genius for seeing a man's interests and pretending, expertly, to share them. Never mind the shape of her nose: what powerful men found so irresistible about Cleopatra was her teasing dark-eyed intensity, the blatancy of her manipulations.

When Antony was fishing, he tried to impress her by attaching pre-caught fish to his line. She wasn't fooled, and the following day she caused a diver to go down and fix a salted fish to the line, which he pulled up amid general hilarity.

He followed her to Alexandria and the pair swanned around in a sensual rout they called the 'Inimitable Livers'. Then came news of the Parthian invasion of Asia Minor and he left her abruptly. But not only was she now pregnant with twins by him; the emotional hook was deeply in Antony.

Three and a half years later, when his marriage to Octavia may have been growing tired, he summoned Cleopatra to

Antioch. The scandal began that was to change the course of history.

Over the next six years, Octavia bore her humiliations with fortitude. But Octavian engaged in furious correspondence with his brother-in-law Antony. His behaviour was not only sexually disreputable. It was politically alarming.

What was he doing, honeying and making love with this foreign queen? What were their intentions? In the minds of some Romans, Cleopatra was a dangerous oriental who had used her charm to befuddle the wits of two Roman generals and restore the Ptolemies in Egypt. But what else did she want?

Some said she wanted to divide the world, with herself as the empress of the east, while her lover ruled in the west. Some said she wanted to come and install herself in Rome so that, as she was reputed to have said, 'my edicts may be read upon the Capitol'.

By 34 BC it was felt that Antony's brain had been softened by ceaseless carnal activity. He was giving away Roman territories to Cleopatra, proclaiming her Queen of Kings and announcing that their children would rule the eastern Roman Empire. He celebrated his triumph over King Artavasdes of Armenia in Alexandria, not Rome. In the eyes of Greeks or Asiatics he was a living Osiris or Dionysus, consort of the goddess-queen of Egypt. It was all getting a bit rum and thoroughly un-Roman.

By 33 BC the triumvirate had been running for ten years and Octavian decided that he had no desire to renew the arrangement. He couldn't face keeping up the pretence of an alliance with Antony. The following year, Antony at last sent for a divorce from Octavia.

In his anger, Octavian decided to break a taboo. He knew that Antony's will was lodged with the Vestal Virgins. He demanded it. They refused. He took it by force and read its contents to the senate. It may have been bad taste to read out a man's will while he was still alive, but the contents were devastating.

Antony's will said that Caesarion was the true heir of Julius Caesar – an affront to Octavian. He was proposing extravagant legacies to his children by Cleopatra. The final insult to the senate and people of Rome: even if he died at Rome, his corpse should be sent to Cleopatra in Alexandria.

Antony was deprived of the consulship.

It was war.

As things turned out, the Battle of Actium was not quite the epic knockdown, drag-out Cecil B. de Mille production that one might have expected. It all went off rather quietly, in fact.

First, the wind blew so hard for four days that battle was impossible. On the fifth day, in perfect conditions, one might have expected Antony's great multi-banked sea-castles to smash forward for freedom. For reasons lost to posterity, he hung back. According to one ancient source, his own flagship was impeded by a sucking fish – which is either some kind of metaphor for his mental state or a very feeble excuse. Eventually his aquatic fortresses lumbered forwards, but they were so undermanned that they could not get it up to ramming speed.

The engagement was evenly matched when Antony's spirit was suddenly broken. For reasons she never explained, Cleopatra's sixty vessels hoisted sail and made straight through the mêlée for the open sea. The enemy watched her with astonishment. As for Antony, says Plutarch, it is said that a lover's soul dwells in the body of another. With the departure of Cleopatra, he lost interest in the fight; he lost interest in everything.

He abandoned the combat and pursued her. She recognized his sails and let him aboard, but for three days he could find nothing to say, to her or anyone else. He sat in the stern with his head in his hands.

Within a year both Antony and Cleopatra were dead, he by his own sword, she by the asp.

If he had stayed with Octavia there seems little question that Antony would have been able to set up some kind of eastern empire, with himself at the head. A role might even have been found for his children with Cleopatra.

If he had kept his head, he would never have brought the foreign queen to Actium. He would never have so antagonized the Roman state that no fewer than 700 senators came with Octavian to the battle, to show loyalty to his cause.

Antony has come down to us as the pre-eminent example of the man who lost it all for lurve. We remember him as the man who became the bellows and the fan to cool a gypsy's lust. Which is exactly how Octavian intended that we should remember him.

As I scrambled with my family around the site of the Battle of Actium we came upon the remnants of Nikopolis, what had once been a vast city, built by Octavian as a memorial to his victory. There was no one else there but a goatherd and his flock. I searched the scene for any kind of inscription or legible memorial, but found nothing. There were brambles and lizards and huge enigmatic islands of red-brick masonry, covered with creepers and rising from the promontory like forgotten Cambodian temples.

But there was nothing to tell you who or what had built this place, and, as I sat there in Gibbonian contemplation, I reflected on the relative durability of great literature and great buildings.

There are at least four famous Latin poems, published in the lifetime of Octavian – or Augustus, as he was about to become

– which celebrate Actium. They have lasted longer and better than the victory city, and the stunning thing is that they all have the same point of view.

They are all, in one way or another, works of Augustan propaganda. Each of them mentions the Egyptian queen; but the name Cleopatra is literally unspeakable. It is left out.

The poets in question are Horace, Virgil and Propertius, and in each case they suggest that there is something quite disgraceful about this woman, and her hold on Antony. She is surrounded by hideous wrinkled eunuchs, says Horace in his ninth *Epode*; and in *Odes* 1.37 he seems to think that her entourage is suffering from sexual diseases or perversions.

Virgil says it is unspeakable that a Roman general should have – horror! – an Egyptian wife, and he describes the woman as playing on her sistrum, wacky foreign musical instrument, while Anubis and other strange Egyptian gods challenge the Roman divinities. Propertius is on much the same lines: 'Roman javelins – ah, the shame! – were grasped by a woman's hand.'

These three Roman poets were writing at ever greater distance from the battle itself: Horace in the same decade, Virgil in the following decade and Propertius in the decade after that. But they are agreed on the epoch-making importance of the event.

'The hands of the world clapped together,' says Propertius, which may or may not be a reference to the geography of the site. Horace says that it is the first time that they can drink Caecuban wine, now that the queen is dead. Virgil has some pretty emetic stuff about how Augustus is standing high in the poop as he enters the battle, with the senate and the people, and with all the gods of Rome.

His very temples are spurting jets of flame, says Virgil, and the star of his father Julius appears at his head.

Now look here, you may ask yourself as you read this stuff. Spurting temples? Stars on his head? These three poets are among the most skilful and imaginative in the history of Western literature. Why are they indulging in this jingoism? Whence this crude xenophobia?

It is, on the face of it, a bit odd that they should all take such violent exception to the fact of Cleopatra's foreignness. Egypt was hardly unknown to the Romans. Virgil makes a fuss about Anubis, and yet the cult of Isis was already well established in the Roman world. All three of them huff and puff about the indignity and shame of Antony's dalliance with an 'Aegyptia coniunx', an Egyptian wife, in Virgil's phrase. But wait a minute.

What about Julius Caesar, whose star appears about the head of his adoptive son? Didn't he have a bit of a stepping out with the queen of Egypt? He most certainly did. And in any case, she wasn't really Egyptian: she was Greek, and Rome was full of Greeks.

So why the moral panic now? We are looking at one of the key reasons why Augustus was so important in the creation of our European culture. Augustus was the first to understand the role of great literature in organizing political opinion, and with the help of Maecenas, his arts supremo, he arrayed about him the most talented and most influential set of poets the world has ever seen.

These poets articulated and propagated a single political consciousness. For most of the next 2,000 years they were to be part of the common culture of Europe.

But in the 400-odd years of the Roman Empire they were even more important. They provided a common literary syllabus and a common attitude to empire. In the east, where they spoke mainly Greek, it would be fair to say that everyone of any culture or standing knew Homer. But wherever Latin was spoken – and that terrain was vast, including both east and west – there were children who for centuries were brought up on Virgil's *Aeneid*, a poem whose avowed intent is to glorify Rome and, incidentally, Augustus.

It is not mere sycophancy that causes the Augustan poets to address the emperor in this fawning way. When Horace says that the air is balmier and the sun shines more sweetly when you are our ruler, O Caesar (i.e. Augustus), he is not being wholly insincere; perhaps not at all insincere.

We should never forget the effect on these men's imaginations of the century that Rome had just been through. From the time of Sulla onwards the streets of Rome had literally run with blood, and since the methods of killing were still so primitive, there was a lot of blood in a Roman death.

When Octavian and the other triumvirs launched their proscriptions in 43 BC, they killed 130 senators and as many as 3,000 knights. Imagine the terror in those households, and even in the households of those who were spared. It was far more homicidal, per capita, than the French Revolution. It was like being a member of the Cambodian bourgeoisie under Pol Pot.

To give you an idea of the culture of brutality that this produced, when Cicero's head was sent to Rome to be nailed to the Speakers' Platform in the Forum it was seized by Fulvia, the first wife of Antony, whose former husband, Clodius, had also been the victim of Cicero's tongue lashings. She sat it on her knees, spat on it, then opened its mouth, pulled out the tongue and pierced it with hairpins.

Horace himself had fought at Philippi in 42 BC (on the wrong side) but he never gives us an account of the carnage. He had no need. Everyone knew what had happened.

Yes, there is something extraordinary and unsettling, to our cynical modern ears, in the panegyrical language with which the Augustan poets discuss their emperor and his achieve-

75

ments. But it is not necessary to think of them as proto-Soviet toadies to the regime. This stuff was heartfelt.

They were living in a society that was increasingly terrified of itself, terrified of the strength and ungovernability of its army and its generals. Across the Roman world and beyond there was a growing sense of not only political but spiritual uncertainty. The idea was gaining ground that one world-epoch was passing away, and another was coming into being, with a new universal ruler who would administer justice and security to the suffering populations of the earth.

In Judaea they were some who would be receptive to the concept of the new Messiah. Rome was by tradition a society that abominated sole rulership. Had they not chucked out their kings? Now they ached so deeply for peace that they were ready to acknowledge that their emperor was a living god, and the Augustan poets said he was.

Be in no doubt that Augustus wanted this stuff. Sometimes he may even have commissioned it directly, though usually through Maecenas. He made these poets rich, and he had a pretty good idea what he wanted them to say. If we look at the Actium poetry we can see how the Augustan authors achieve two propaganda objectives that were essential for creating that sense of unity in the Roman world – the unity that Augustus achieved, which lasted for so long, and which post-Romans have found so difficult to replicate.

First there is the exaltation of the central figure of the emperor. It will be one of the themes of this book that it is very hard to create a single European political consciousness without such a figure.

Then there is the notion of the outsider, the external threat. There are few more potent forces for unity than the notion that we all face the same collective peril. That is why the poets all make such a big deal of the alarming foreignness of Cleopatra. Like so many other right-wing authoritarian rulers, Augustus sought to justify his emergency powers by constantly reminding the public of the twin threats, at home (civil war) and abroad (Cleopatra, the Parthians, Arminius, the hairy Germans, whatever) that only he could deal with.

To reiterate: these are great poets, not clunking propagandists. There is more than a touch of admiration for Cleopatra in Horace 1.37, as he describes her suicide, her refusal to flee. Much of the genius of Virgil's *Aeneid* lies in the sympathy with which he describes those who must die in the cause of building Rome: Dido, the African queen whom Aeneas loves and leaves; Turnus, the Latin ruler whom he slaughters in the last lines of the epic. We are meant to feel shattered at their tragedy, and we do.

But in magnifying the tragic importance of the victims of Rome, Virgil accomplishes his primary task, which is to magnify the importance of Rome. In fact he provides a manifesto of world domination. As Anchises says to his son Aeneas, the hero of the epic and the founder of Rome,

> Tu regere imperio populos, Romane, memento
> (hae tibi erunt artes), pacisque imponere morem;
> parcere subiectis et debellare superbos.

'Remember, Roman, to rule with the rod of empire – these shall be your arts – and to impose the way of peace, to spare the vanquished and war down the proud.'

That was telling them.

In the late nineteenth century Lord Bryce found in Virgil the perfect embodiment of the spirit of liberal imperialism. He was 'the national poet in whom the spirit of empire found its highest expression'. And yet Virgil is so many-textured that

American students could read him in the 1960s and believe that he was somehow against the Vietnam War. Turnus died for peace, man. The early Christian fathers believed that he was a seer, who had miraculously foretold the gospel. For a long time it was seen as a serious defect of Christianity that, as a pagan, Virgil could find no place in heaven. Dante makes him his guide in the Underworld. T. S. Eliot says he was the rock on which Europe's civilization was built.

So venerated was this Mantuan poet that for centuries it was the custom to flip open his works at random and read the 'sortes Virgilianae' – a sort of horoscope based on whatever Virgil happened to be on about where your finger hit the page. Charles I consulted the sortes before the Battle of Naseby and they looked pretty bleak. What is it about this man's language that convinced people there was magic in the web of it?

It is hard to know how to persuade a non-Latinist, as I impertinently assume the reader to be. But try this line, from Book Six of the Aeneid, in which the poet describes Aeneas and Co. heading for the Underworld: 'Ibant obscuri sola sub nocte per umbras.' You don't really have to know Latin to see roughly what that must mean. 'They went in darkness under the lonely night sky through the shadows' is a literal translation, but it hardly does justice to the slow, spine-tingling spookiness of the original.

There was a time when every man and woman of education in Europe would have known that line. In the nineteenth century Virgil was seldom off the lips of British parliamentarians. Here is Lord Brougham, spouting the famous description of the monster Fama:

Parva metu primo, mox sese attollit in auras
ingrediturque solo et caput inter nubile condit.

'At first small from timidity, but soon rising to giant size, her feet on the earth but her head in the clouds.'

He was speaking of the recent invention called income tax, which, he prophesied with Virgilian accuracy, would grow ever bigger. Ho ho ho.

If that shared understanding of the poet was still alive a 100 years ago, think of the impact he had on the Roman Empire. Virgil and the other Augustan poets were themselves the disseminators of the Latin language, and it was not just the message – pride in Rome – that they communicated. It was the medium itself, the Latin language, with its quality of clicking together sweetly and unforgettably like perfectly dressed blocks of stone: that was in itself an agent of cultural integration. Think how Latin works, with its ruthless laws of inflection and agreement, and the way it must have assimilated the mental processes of the peoples of Europe. It wasn't just what Virgil was saying that turned people into Romans; it was the way he said it.

I think back to my own time at a European school in Brussels and the total absence of a common syllabus in either history or literature.

Whichever way you look at it, Waterloo will always mean something very different to a Briton and a Frenchman.

Across the Roman world the name Actium meant the same thing. It had one single, clear, immutable political value, and that was the achievement of Virgil and the Augustan poets, and above all it was the achievement of Augustus.

What can we in modern Europe do, deprived as we are of a propaganda genius like Augustus, and long ago bereft of our single political consciousness?

Well, I have a proposal for the Eurocrats. If you want to rebuild a common European culture you must go back to its roots, and I propose that we begin, very modestly, with a single book of the *Aeneid,* a single book that every child in the European Union would have to read by the time he or she was sixteen, so that they would not only have something in common with each other – and something beautiful, at that – but also something in common with the age when Europe was last united.

Augustine said he wept more for the death of Dido than he did for the death of his own saviour. What about Book Four, the best book of the best poem of the best poet?

Augustus was in one sense only building on the achievements of untold numbers of Roman imperialists who conquered and Romanized so much of Europe, the Near East and Africa. But he added an extra dimension: not just that the empire was divine, but that there was a new semi-divine figurehead at the centre of it all. It is time to consider the growth of Roman imperial theology and the extraordinary parallel growth in Christian theology. I hope to show that this last can be seen as a reaction to – and rejection of – the cult of the emperor and the values of Rome.

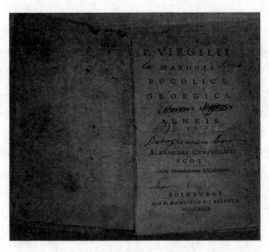

Thomas Jefferson's boyhood copy of Virgil

CHAPTER FOUR

Augustus Caesar and Jesus Christ

This is a detail from the Ara Pacis, the altar of peace, that was dedicated in 9 BC to celebrate the achievement of Augustus in the Gaulish and Spanish campaigns. We see Augustus and the rest of the imperial family, carved in Parian marble, and attired for a sacrifice: the women modestly hooded, the men with wreaths. The whole thing is a perfect picture of piety. The trouble with the imperial system was that neither Augustus' family nor his descendants were as wise, modest or restrained as the first and greatest emperor of Rome.

Let us begin with the coincidences.

No, they aren't entirely coincidences. They can't be.

81

Let us begin with the eerie similarities between the language used to describe the advent of Jesus Christ and the rise to power of Augustus.

Forty years before Jesus was born, and when Augustus was already consul, Virgil wrote a poem which has earned him the status of a kind of pagan saint.

It is the fourth, or so-called Messianic, *Eclogue*, and when the early Christians looked back at it they could scarcely believe it. This greatest of the Roman poets appears to prophesy the coming of the Saviour – in language that is uncannily like that of the Bible.

There is going to be a new golden age, says Virgil in the messianic *Eclogue*. The creator of this age will be a wonder child. He will free mankind from sin and pacify and rule the world. It's going to be heavenly, he says. 'The goats will come home by themselves with milk-filled udders. Nor will the cattle be in fear of great lions ... The serpent will perish, and the treacherous herb of poison will perish.'

Sound familiar? It's just like Isaiah, isn't it? It was an important part of the gospel stories that the coming of Christ should be in fulfilment of the ancient prophecies of the Old Testament. So the New Testament evangelists quote Isaiah, to give their account more weight.

This is what Isaiah had said, seven hundred years earlier: 'The people that walked in darkness have seen a great light ... For unto us a child is born, unto us a son is given: and the government shall be upon his shoulder, and his name shall be called Wonderful, Counsellor, the Mighty God, the Everlasting Father, the Prince of Peace' (Isaiah 9.2, 6).

And he goes on to prophesy: 'The wolf shall also dwell with the lamb, and the leopard shall lie down with the kid; and the calf and the young lion and the fatling together; and a little child shall lead them ... And the sucking child shall play on the whole of the asp, and the weaned child shall put his hand on the cockatrice' den' (Isaiah 11.6–9).

Now what is going on here? Why is Virgil apparently echoing Jewish prophets, and using rhapsodical language about a child being born, but decades before the event? We must assume, I fear, that he was not in fact a pre-Christian prophet of the coming of Christ.

There are other sensible theories about how Virgil came to echo Isaiah, and to anticipate the gospels. It may well be that he was inspired by Jewish ideas of golden ages and messiahs, transmitted to the west in the 'Sibylline oracles', a mixture of Greek and Jewish religious arcana.

The interesting question is what Virgil was on about. Who was this wonder child? The obvious answer is surely that it was the stripling wunderkind, Octavian.

Like the other Augustan poets, Virgil had grown up amid the horrors of the civil war. So desperately did people hope for peace that they were prepared to attribute divinity to anyone who could make the misery end.

Of course, it is laying it on a bit thick to call Octavian a divine wonder child; but then look at Horace. He tells us with a straight face in the *Odes* that Augustus is Mercury, come down to earth to restore order after Roman brother has been slaughtering brother: 'May you return late to heaven, and long may you stay with joy among the Roman people,' says Horace of Octavian, this chill and subtle terrorist, who was already rich on the property of men he had killed.

This joyful youthful divinity was in truth a ruthless, blood-soaked dynast. Among his war crimes was the slaughter of 300 men after the Battle of Perusia, as a sacrifice to the shade of Julius Caesar. And yet in another place Horace says that Augustus is a living Jupiter, a present god on earth, who will add Parthia and even Britain to the empire.

Horace and Virgil are not potty with ruler worship; they are not blind. But they are giving poetic expression to a deep and typically Roman feeling that the gods must be angry with Rome: there can be no other explanation of the disasters that have befallen society. And only the gods can redeem the place.

Which is why they are so ready to break with precedent and ascribe divinity to Augustus. In case there is any doubt about the identity of this Roman saviour, Virgil spells it out in the *Aeneid*. The Sibyl sees Augustus in the underworld, and refers to her own prophecies – by which we may understand Virgil to mean his own earlier poem, the messianic *Eclogue*. She says: 'This is the man, this is he, whom you have often heard promised: Augustus Caesar, descendant of a god, who will again establish the golden ages that once reigned in the fields of Latium under Saturn of old, and who will carry forward empire over the Garamantes and Indians.'

So there we are. Decades before the birth of Jesus Christ, these are some of the things that Roman poets are saying about the advent of Augustus: that he is a saviour, that he will redeem his people, that he will dwell among us for a time and then return to heaven, and above all that his function is to expiate the sins of his people – in this case civil war. Oh yes: one other point – Augustus is the son of God.

Julius Caesar was deified on his death, and from 42 BC onwards his adoptive son was known as Divi Filius, which means Son of God.

Within the same period of fifty years, the same phenomenon crops up in two ancient and proud civilizations, the Romans and the Jews. For centuries they had scorned the grovellings of Hellenistic ruler cults. Their rulers were men, not gods. The Romans were deeply hostile to the idea of kingship, let alone a divine ruler. As for the orthodox Jews, there was no god but Yahweh.

Is it really a coincidence that in the same short space of time both cultures are visited by a man who bucks tradition and calls himself the son of God? Is it really sensible to say that the Roman experience had no influence on the Christian story?

And that is not the end of the amazing similarities between the story of Augustus and the gospel narratives. Suetonius tells us that the senate is supposed to have declared a ban on the rearing of male babies during the year in which Augustus was born, because of a prophecy that an infant king would be brought into the world that year. The story is nonsense, of course. But does it not sound freakily similar to the story of Herod's 'slaughter of the innocents'?

Then we are told that Octavian's mother, Atia, had a dream, during a visit to the temple of Apollo, that she had been favoured by a visit from the god in the form of a snake. Her child had been born nine months later. That's right: it's a pre-Christian version of the Annunciation. Blessed art thou Atia among women, and blessed is the fruit of thy womb Octavian.

... And Atia said, 'How can this be, for I know not a man? Wait a mo: it was Apollo the snake god.'

Or listen to the evangelical fervour with which the province of Asia decides, in 9 BC, to celebrate the birthday of Augustus. The assembly had offered an award for the best honour proposed to Augustus, and the winner was the man who proposed to make the emperor's birthday – 23 September – New Year's Day in the local Greek calendar. Great idea! says the assembly:

... the divine Caesar's birthday, which we might justly consider equal to the beginning of all things.
He has given a different appearance to the whole world,

which would happily have gone to utter ruin, had not Caesar been born to the common good fortune of mankind. Therefore each of us would justly reckon his birthday to be the beginning of his own life, since that day was the end of regretting that we had been born.

Hark at the Christianizing language of the decree – nine years before Christ was born. The assembly describes the wheeze as '*euangelia*' – good tidings, gospels – and says 'the beginning of good tidings for the world was the birthday of the god'.

Augustus' lucky sign was Capricorn, in celebration of the date of his conception. What was the date of his conception, when Atia was blessed by the visitation of snaky old Apollo? It was 23 December … which strikes me as being spookily close to Christmas.

So what do you think happened when the gospel writers came to tell the story of Jesus? Do you think they were influenced by the idea of a son of god that had suffused the entire Roman Empire, including Judaea? Of course they were.

That is not a blasphemous suggestion – or not necessarily a blasphemous suggestion. To say that the Christmas story need not be wholly true or original is, after all, the position of most Anglican bishops. It is not fatal to Christianity, or not necessarily fatal. All I mean is that we cannot make complete sense of Christ's ministry and message unless we understand the Roman context – political and cultural – in which he appeared.

Jesus was a Jew in first century Galilee. It was part of a Roman client kingdom in a world dominated by Rome. As we hear in the gospel every Christmas, he only happened to be born in a manger in Bethlehem because of a decree of Caesar

Augustus that all the world should be taxed, which meant that Mary and Joseph had to leave Nazareth and turn up for the census – the assessment of their assets – in Bethlehem.

But Judaea was not quite like the other provinces, and the Jews had a very particular view of themselves and of their religion. They weren't like the toadies of the province of Asia, dribbling with joy at the notion of turning the emperor's birthday into New Year's Day. They had a God called Yahweh. They were not allowed to mention his name, let alone make graven images of him. Not only did they have no other god before him – they had no other god at all. Nope: the Romans were happy to worship any number of gods, including, now, their emperor. But any such concession was unthinkable for the Jews.

In fact, the Jews were so stroppy that they were constantly revolting; and before he went off to get massacred in the German forests, our old friend Publius Quintilius Varus was in charge of crucifying thousands of Jewish zealots for their general obstreperousness.

In the end this refusal to assimilate led to the sacking of Jerusalem and the destruction of the temple in AD 70. But during the period of Christ's ministry, it was clearly the strategy of the Jewish establishment to make an accommodation with the Romans. They did their best to ignore the great unbridgeable gap between themselves and the occupying power: ever since Augustus, it had been a doctrine of the Roman Empire that the emperor was divine.

When Virgil and Horace said Augustus was divine, it was partly heartfelt, partly just a *façon de parler*. They actually knew the man. They didn't think he was literally a god, in the sense that Jupiter was a god. But with time and distance the cult of the emperor became ever more serious and sincere.

From Spain to Gaul, from Germany to Africa to Asia to

Greece, there were educated people who were prepared to accept that he was *divi filius*, the son of god.

Now how did that square with the Christian claims? Jesus was not only the son of God. He was *the* only son of God.

It was a recipe for trouble.

To put it at its most schematic, the two contemporary 'sons of god' – Jesus and Augustus – were to institute or at least articulate two rival value systems. For centuries they coexisted, until the one was finally superimposed on the other.

Christianity triumphed, but it was largely thanks to the imagination of Augustus that the Roman imperial method lasted for so long; and it was the success of the imperial system that made Christianity possible.

The deeper one looks into Augustus and his doings, the more stupendous his achievement appears. This pale, thin, frog-like young man stamped his personality on the entire Roman world. What was going on behind that bulging brow, with the blond locks artfully arranged in a fringe?

He was a small man, and that is sometimes an explanation for ambition. As a young man, he seems to have had a healthy sexual appetite, peremptorily leading the wives of other men out of dinner parties after which they returned breathless and flushed and their hair dishevelled. And yet he was no sensualist, not by the standards of Antony. His later years were filled with social legislation of the most eye-watering Puritanism.

He wanted poetry to be written about his reign, and had the genius to see the potential for propaganda of the circle around Maecenas. But you couldn't call him a *littérateur*. We have his own account of his labours, the *res gestae divi Augusti*, but they do not match the literary elegance of Julius Caesar, his adoptive father, whose self-glorifying account of the Gallic War is a piece of exemplarily lucid Latin.

He became fantastically rich, and owned more and more

land on the Palatine Hill – the hill of the palaces, above the Forum. But by later standards his dwelling was very modest, and he lived in the same small brick room for forty years.

He went through an elaborate pretence, once he had seized supreme power, of being nothing more constitutionally significant than *primus inter pares*. He would enact a great rigmarole of pretending not to want his various positions of power; and, of course, when they all begged him, O Caesar, to be so kind as to rule over us, he gracefully condescended to do so.

What he possessed, perhaps more than anyone else in Roman history, was an understanding of how to get and keep power. He understood the deep sheep-like human need for leadership, what Hitler called *Führerprinzip*, and he grasped the psychological tricks needed to create that extraordinary sense of personal identification between the masses and the ruler.

The reign of Augustus teaches us something rather frightening about society, and about what human beings will accept from their rulers. There he is, at the very start of the Roman imperial system that was to be the template of all succeeding empires, and what does he show? That you can institute a regime that is on the whole less free, less democratic, more tyrannical than what went before – and still be hailed eternally as the author of a golden age.

Like all Roman politicians he made a great thing about restoring the 'republic', the old and complicated system of voting, and the limits on magisterial power, to which it was pious to attribute the success of Rome. In reality, he hollowed out that system until it was a shell and the votes of the people were valueless.

Elections carried on, but the way it worked in Rome was that you needed a certain popular acclaim to get elected. The route to people's hearts was public munificence or ostentation – building a set of new baths, for instance, or laying on games of stunning bloodthirstiness. Slowly and stealthily, Augustus clamped down on the ambitions of other great men and invisibly blocked the old paths to advancement.

In 29 BC one Marcus Licinius Crassus claimed a right Roman triumph for his actions in Thrace. The proconsul of Macedonia had killed the enemy chief with his own hand! Tremendous. According to ancient Roman rules, he was entitled to strip his victim of his armour and make a kind of ritual sacrifice of the equipment at a temple in Rome. It was a classic piece of Roman swanking, and likely to be accompanied by huge public interest. The dedication of these shields, baldrics and greaves was known as the *spolia opima*, and the really exciting thing about the *spolia opima* was that they had not been awarded for hundreds of years.

The practice had traditionally been started by Romulus in about 750 BC, when he killed King Acron of Caenina in a duel. Since then only two men had pulled off the feat: Cornelius Cossus, who killed Lars Tolumnius of Veii in 437 BC, and M. Claudius Marcellus, who killed the Celtic chieftain Viridomarus in 222 BC.

One can imagine how Augustus must have sucked his teeth at the news of Crassus' success. Of course, he was the victor of Actium and had just celebrated a huge triumph in honour of his defeat of Antony and Cleopatra. But deep down he was always a little insecure of his own military reputation, and this exultant Crassus might possibly be a nuisance – or at least detract from his own glory.

There would be street parties and bunting, he realized. The lascivious matrons of Rome would make much of this general, and offer to have his babies. And, as he divined, the real trouble with the celebration of the *spolia opima* was not just that Crassus was bringing glory on the house of Crassus;

the victory was bringing glory on Rome – and it was a vital part of Augustus' political analysis that as far as possible he, and he alone, should be associated with the glory of Rome.

So he came up with a wheeze. A lesser politician would simply have had Crassus bumped off and incurred the resulting unpopularity. Augustus was more subtle. He understood his people, and their obsession with tradition, and the validation of the past, and the importance of being able to show that whatever was being done now was correct because it was in some way what had always been done.

That was why he lived right next to an old hut, which he claimed was the very hut in which Romulus had lived; and being a terrific antiquarian he was able to rummage around and produce an ancient linen corslet, or vest, on which it was written that Cossus – he who had been awarded the *spolia opima* in 437 BC – had been consul at the time. Aha, said Augustus: that was very, very important. It showed that you could only celebrate this particular form of triumph if you were the commander of the army, and it so happened that he, Augustus, was commander of the army, whereas Marcus Crassus was just a proconsul.

So so-rree, Marcus! No *spolia* for you. It's the ancient custom, said Augustus, and everyone tugged their forelocks, subdued by the irrefutable proof of a 400-year-old vest. By the next decade, triumphs had been abolished altogether for everyone except members of the imperial house; and though other people were allowed to be consul, Augustus had what was called *maius imperium* – the greater power.

Rome was built by the exertions of a citizen army, in which every adult male was expected to do military service. It was the culture that produced not only Rome's fabulous conquests, but also the hardy and independent spirit of Rome's mutually antagonistic generals and their taste for civil war. Augustus changed that. He effectively professionalized the army, fixed rates of pay and length of service; above all, he decided that the troops should make an oath of loyalty not to Rome, but to himself. At a stroke he had turned the army into a thing apart – no longer an emanation of the will of the Roman people, but the chief and irresistible accessory of imperial power.

It had hitherto been unthinkable – in theory – for troops to appear in the city itself. As Augustus' reign went on, the sight became more and more common, until by the end the Praetorian Guard was established on the outskirts of the city.

For a long time you could tell from a distance if Augustus was coming down the street, because he would be surrounded by all twenty-four *lictors* – the officials who carried the *fasces*, the bundles of rods that symbolized authority. Though for many years he was technically co-ruler with another consul, the other chap had no lictors or fasces at all, and his own procession must have looked decidedly thin.

Augustus was cunning, and he knew that his tyranny would be all the more effective for maintaining a democratic façade, and so there came a moment when he disavowed the consulship. Let others have a go, he said. But he always kept his own special mixture of republican prerogatives, the *maius imperium*, as well as the powers of a tribune – which gave him the presidential power of veto, and made his person sacrosanct. He retained control of the provinces, and power slowly flowed away from other Romans and towards the palace on the hill.

He instituted a crackdown on other means by which notables might suck up to the public. He capped spending on the games, for instance, for everyone except himself, and he was responsible for games of such mounting extravagance that over the next few centuries Roman appetites for slaughter were to have an irreversible impact on the ecosystem of Africa, more or less denuding the savannah of species. And unlike some of the more fastidious republican spirits, Augustus was smart enough to attend the games in person, visibly delighting in the pleasures of the people, just as any ambitious modern demagogue is obliged to take joy in football.

Earlier in Augustus' reign it had been common for Roman grandees to erect big and magnificent buildings, that men might admire them and their philanthropy. By the end of his reign – and he reigned a very long time, forty-five years – all such major public works in Rome were identified with the state, and with the emperor.

If you want an index of the difference between democratic Athens and imperial Rome, consider the way we think of their respective artistic achievements. We have the Parthenon of Phidias, Ictinus and Callicrates – the sculptors themselves, who were allowed to be individually famous in democratic Athens. From Rome we have the Ara Pacis of Augustus, the baths of Caracalla, the palace of Domitian: the artists and architects have been lost to memory, squeezed out by the dominance of the emperor, the job that Augustus created.

Augustus said that he 'found Rome of brick and left it of marble'. That may be an exaggeration, but it was certainly in his reign that production at the Carrara quarries went into a roar, and that bright white marble, together with dazzling coloured stones and modified Corinthian columns, created an Augustan vernacular that spread around the world.

Under Augustus, the Roman habit of lapidary inscription becomes suddenly more graceful, the characters straighter and sharper, and usually inked in with red. What we are looking at is an Augustan style, a brand. Like Albert Speer, Augustus understood that his regime should have a characteristic visual impact on the population, and that Augustan brand was imitated across the empire.

He insisted on a particular style of dress – the toga – in spite of what we can now see as its obvious Darwinian inferiority to trousers. Virgil, the poet of Roman imperial triumph, calls the Romans the 'toga'ed people', the *gens togata*. Augustus was a martinet for certain habits and standards, in a way that seems quite loopy to our modern taste.

It is one of the boasts of the Roman Empire that they ran this vast territory, for centuries, with very few officials and a pretty minimalist approach to regulation. By and large it is true that the Roman state was unobtrusive; but we must make an exception for the moral reforms of Augustus. These began in about 18 BC and they represent an attempt by the emperor to peer into the bedrooms of Rome that seems creepy to the point of madness. Adultery was to be punished by exile. Indeed, a man could be prosecuted by the state for *failing* to sue his own wife if he caught her having sex with another man. Obediently some of the Augustan poets begin to chant the chorus of this moral backlash. In his third book of *Odes*, Horace starts raving about how respectable Roman matrons are having it away with Spanish trawler captains. From a man who is normally so urbane, it is all very distressing to read.

In the earlier books of *Odes*, the poet is to be heard lusting after trembling young fillies and heifers, and remarking that it is time they were broken in by the old bull Horace, and all that kind of thing. Now he happily blasts the moral foghorn of Augustus. Young girls! he honks. All they think about these days is sex, sex, sex! He sounds like some *Daily Mail* columnist after a particularly difficult tube ride.

These laws were not very popular and not easy to enforce, and they were a licence for hypocrisy on an imperial scale. It was still expressly permitted, of course, for a Roman man to have any kind of liaison with anyone who was not a married Roman woman – and that meant all sorts of wenching with slave girls and prostitutes of a kind that is no doubt accurately depicted by the BBC's various series on Rome.

If a married Roman woman wanted to keep up her adulterous relationship, she could get round the law by the demented expedient of going to the *aediles* and registering herself as a prostitute – a loophole that Tiberius, Augustus' successor, was forced to close when it became embarrassingly popular with the wives of senators. We yearn to ask why Augustus thought it right to meddle in this way. The answer, says Professor Andrew Wallace-Hadrill, Director of the British School in Rome, is all to do with control, and I am sure he is right.

He says it is a bit like the Catholic Church, in that if you set up a series of requirements and prescriptions about people's most deeply felt urges and instincts, then you control them in a profound and lasting way. In making decisions about the most intimate and personal aspects of their lives, they find they must deal with you, the emperor: and that puts the emperor in a position of immense power.

The next question is, why did people put up with it? Why did people so readily tolerate this political, cultural and moral dictatorship?

We are drawn back to the civil wars and the deep collective sense in Rome that their society was not just sick, but guilty. They needed and deserved peace, but they could see that they would have to pay a price. The Augustan settlement, with its flagrant erosion of democracy, was a price worth paying. Above all, they accepted the Augustan settlement because of the brilliant sleight of hand by which he managed so fully and perfectly to identify his own dignity, glory and authority with the dignity, glory and authority of Rome.

In the optimism that followed the civil wars he created a new creed of Roman greatness. That greatness was suggested everywhere: by grand poetry, by new buildings, by the victories over the Swiss and German tribes, and all these things were explicitly associated with Augustus. It was accepted that the success of Rome was divinely ordained, and it was accepted that the Roman emperor was also divine.

It wasn't just in Asia that Augustus was hailed as a god, though ruler worship was certainly easiest in the Greek cities with a tradition of such devotion. The divinity of the emperor was agreed across the empire, in Spain and France and Germany. Local elites vied for offices in the cult of Augustus. In a way that seems quite incredible to modern sensibilities, temples were built to him, sacrifices were made.

I was standing in the huge Roman theatre in Orange, in southern France, and had an insight into the way Augustus fed himself into your imaginative processes. Suppose you have just watched some magnificent drama, and you are all breathless and stunned at the end, and full of the correct Aristotelian emotions of pity and fear. You look up at the proscenium as you file out, and there he is, arm aloft like Shane Warne doing his flipper, effulgent in marble and larger than life. He is with you at the theatre, in your moments of deepest aesthetic feeling; he is with you in the games, when your soul is harrowed by the carnage of men and animals.

Above all, he is with you at the moment of sacrifice and propitiation to the gods. The cult of Augustus was taken so seriously that the very priests would have his face sewn on the tops of their cowls, just as the women of Malawi would have the face of Hastings Kamuzu Banda emblazoned on each buttock; except in the Roman case the occasion was truly sacred, not merely political.

His name or image was to be found on innumerable statues, columns, arches, altars, and in all manner of rituals and ceremonials. Across the empire, parish magistrates were called Augustales, and the jobs were filled by the richest and most successful ex-slaves. In case you failed to catch his name it was used for city after city across the empire, from Augusta Praetoria (Aosta, in Italy) to Augusta Treverorum (Trier, in Germany) Caesaraugusta (Zaragoza, in Spain) and beyond.

Until the age of Augustus, different states and cities produced their own coin. For a time he even kept up the practice of allowing distinguished Romans to mint their own currency. By the end of his reign, the head of the emperor was more or less universal, and not just on the currency. It was more pervasive than the image of Kemal Atatürk in Turkey (and that is to be found in every sub-post office, every public convenience and every municipal car pound in modern Turkey). It was more pervasive than the image of Mao in China or Kim Il-Sung in North Korea. It was thought quite fitting that in the dining rooms of sophisticated families there should be a marble portrait bust of the emperor.

Imagine the frisson of horror if you went out to dinner in Islington and looked up to see a marble rendition of Blair, or Thatcher, or even John Major. You'd think it was either a joke or a demented piece of idolatry.

The Romans thought their ruler cult was neither frivolous nor idolatrous, but a serious statement of their allegiance to Rome, to the idea of Rome, to the greatest power and civilization on earth which – and this is the key point – was divinely incarnated in this man.

Which brings us back to Jesus and the problem he created. The nub of his message was that there was a distinction between the kingdom of heaven and a world run by Rome. 'Render unto Caesar the things that are Caesar's, and unto God the things that are God's,' he says. That sounds like common sense to us. Make a separation, he seems to be saying, between religion and politics. Quite right, too.

But it was a crucial part of the Augustan settlement that

there was no distinction between religion and politics. To understand how the Romans ran Europe so well for so long, we have to understand the mesmerizing way in which Augustus set up the idea of a divinely ordained empire, with a divinely ordained emperor at the centre.

For Jesus to hold up one of Caesar's coins and say there was nothing divine about the emperor – now that was actually offensive to Roman ears. That was Romano-scepticism. That was verging on blasphemy.

And that was really what the Jewish leaders, the Sanhedrin, disliked most about Jesus. Not so much that he claimed he was the son of God; there was nothing especially blasphemous about such a claim. What they feared was that he would cause trouble with the Romans. That is why they handed him over to the Romans to be crucified. He was a political liability.

As John reports it, the Pharisees say to themselves: 'If we let him thus alone, all men will believe in him, and the Romans shall come and take away our place and our nation.'

They couldn't risk that and so he died; and Christ's martyrdom became the central act of a religion that was, on the face of it, intentionally antithetical to Roman values. Of course we must be careful not to generalize too wildly.

Doubtless the Roman world was full of meek, pious, selfless pagan Romans, brimming with brotherly love, just as there are and always have been untold numbers of licentious, hypocritical glory-hungry Christians.

But, broadly speaking, I hope you will accept that the two 'sons of God' – Augustus and Christ – instantiated two very different ethical systems. There was the Roman view of what it meant to lead the good life, in which the afterlife was not a very important element, but which focused hard on glory, ostentation and honour. In so far as the pagan Romans believed in immortality, they looked to the deathless renown of poetry, or battlefield honours, or great buildings in which their name might be up there on the entablature.

Then there was the Christian view, which tended at least in principle to dismiss earthly pleasures and triumphs in favour of the life of the world to come.

The great advantage of the Roman system was that their emperor-god actually existed. Unlike Mercury, Jupiter or Hercules, you could see this god. If you made it to Rome, you might watch him pass by, or touch the hem of his garment. This had enormous political advantages, and it helps to explain how the Romans ran Europe and created that sense of unity that has eluded everyone else ever since. In the imperial cult, Augustus made a single channel, a confluence, for people's religious and patriotic feelings. Of course, he was not the only god, nor by any means the most important god. But his cult was a way of expressing loyalty to him and to Rome.

And yet the fact of his physical existence was also, of course, the eventual cause of the downfall of the imperial system and of the creed itself.

Even as Augustus was promulgating his fierce moral laws, his relations were letting the side down. His daughter, Julia, was caught in the Forum itself, performing unmentionable acts with married men. (Asked about the surprising resemblance between her children and her husband, she quipped, 'I only take passengers when the boat is already fully'.) She was banished. His wife, Livia, became a byword for stepmotherly viciousness and intrigue. The eventual problem was that the family of the emperor was uncontrollable, and that so few of Augustus' successors had a fraction of his gifts.

In the long run, the behaviour of some emperors was to become so disgusting that their claims to divinity looked pretty feeble.

In the end the Christian system was to prevail, when Constantine had the wit to convert.

But it was the pagan system, with emperor worship at its heart, that allowed the Romans to run Europe for so long. Augustus had the imagination to see how it might work, and the authority to fulfil the role so successfully that it was centuries before it finally fell apart.

The emperor cult was a key element in the process by which Europe was Romanized, but by no means the only trick the Romans played. It is time now to look at how they transformed most of the known world, and persuaded the peoples of the Mediterranean, Europe and much of the Near East that they would be mad not to want to be Roman.

They started with one huge ideological advantage.

PART THREE

How the Romans Did It

CHAPTER FIVE

Citizens

Romulus prepares to seize a Sabine woman and turn her into a
Roman. Later on, people across the empire longed to be Roman.

Between the ages of eight and eleven I was educated at a
marvellous place in Brussels called the European School. It is
one of the few schools in the world that is avowedly political,
rather than religious, in its core dogma. It has a message for its
pupils. Somewhere in the grounds is a plaque bearing the
words of Jean Monnet, founder of the European Community,
in which he speaks of his hopes for the little children who

gambol around, screaming and yelling in the umpteen official languages of the EU. 'May they become in mind European,' he says, and drones on about how he hopes they will come out of the school resolved to build a common European fatherland.

Well, it didn't work on me. And my overriding impression is that it didn't really work on any of the other children there, either. In the primary school, at least, there was a firm principle of apartheid between the various language groups, or 'sections', as they were called. The British played with the British, very occasionally drafting in a Dutch or a Danish kid, provided they could speak the language. The French might conceivably hobnob with the Italians, though not much, and – I shouldn't say this, but who cares – I am afraid the Germans played more or less exclusively with other Germans.

And then when I came back to Brussels as a journalist in the late 1980's, I found that it was the same system among the grown-ups. In the press room of the Berlaymont, the home of the European Commission, the Spanish journalists would form their own little huddle, and receive their own briefings from their own ministers about their own national points of interest (usually nabbing British fish). They would all have a particularly Spanish aspect, with natty sports jackets, cigarettes and well-trimmed beards. The Germans would go into their huddle; the Brits would make a spinney of their own. It was all deeply dispiriting for the federalists; and after work the pattern of segregation was even worse.

There were British dinner parties, at which British expats talked about British schools, and the difficulty of finding Weetabix and Marmite in supermarkets. Very occasionally, as in the playground, these events would be leavened by the addition of a token Frenchman or Dutch girl; but on the whole I am afraid it was the same all around Brussels, with members of the language groups retreating into their own drawing rooms and dining rooms, and gabbling in their mother tongues about the other nations, and how generally impossible they were.

I would be very surprised if it has changed in the ten years since I left; and indeed it appears that the rhetoric of the modern EU has been adjusted to suit this uncomfortable reality. We are always being told nowadays that 'the nation-state is the building block' of Europe.

There, of course, we have the biggest and profoundest difference between our world and the Roman world, a difference whose causes and consequences are likely to concern politicians for generations to come. The Roman Empire occupied a territory that now comprises thirty separate nation-states, some of them still capable of pretty strident mutual rhetorical antagonism.

And yet the elites of the Roman Empire behaved in a completely different way from the elites of modern Brussels. They would have been shocked to find that after 2,000 years leading figures from the province of Britannia no longer had dinner with people from the province of Hispania, let alone from Gallia or Italia. They would have been appalled at this petty-minded balkanization, this jabbering in strange creoles, some of them reminiscent of Latin, some less so, some not reminiscent at all.

To understand how Rome held our forefathers together so effectively and for so long, we need to understand a key point of Roman ideology. To trace the earliest origins of this notion, I went to see a man who was digging a hole in the middle of the Roman Forum. His name was Professor Andrea Carandini and he looked like some archaeologist from an Agatha Christie novel, all dandified in a linen jacket and panama hat; and on the face of it his mission seemed faintly barmy.

It would be fair to say that Professor Carandini is a deeply venerated figure in the world of Roman archaeology, but one whose aims and methods are now thought to be increasingly controversial. He told me that he regards himself as a *flamen*, a priest of the temples he is investigating, and there is something dizzying – even to the layman – about the certainty of his assertions.

It was a hot day in the Forum, and the heart of what had once been the Roman Empire was full of slack-faced tourists. Sitting exhausted on a tumbledown capital, a man from Liverpool said he found the whole thing incomprehensible and disappointing, and was going straight back to his cruise ship. It was nothing but a load of ruins, he said.

But around the Carandini excavation there was a buzz of excitement, as other tourists pressed their faces up against the wire mesh that surrounded the dig. 'There,' said the old Italian fossicker, who had been speaking in beautiful English to me, 'there you can see the line of rubbish and burning which means we are back to the eighth century.' I followed the direction of his finger, down into the hole, and I must confess that I felt a real ping of fascination. Could he possibly be right? Everyone seemed to agree about the carbon dating. It just depended on whether you believed he had rightly attributed the building he had found.

'There are the post holes of the palace of the kings,' he said, and produced a picture of his discovery. It seemed to be a long bungalow with various people lounging around with sticks. I offered that it looked a bit like a Surrey golf club, and it is a measure of Professor Carandini's courtliness that he did not miss a beat.

'Yes,' he said, 'or like the palace of King Arthur, no?' We were looking, he said, at something that may well have been the palace of the man who founded Rome itself. My dear Mr

Johnson, said the visionary Italian excavator, this could have been the palace of Romulus.

Yes, I got a prickle in the nape of my neck as I looked 6 or 7 feet down to the bottom of the hole, and realized I was looking at the very beginnings of Rome. There was a girl in a hat, slowly and carefully sweeping and sponging at a patch of mud. Rising up the excavated wall of mud to her left I could clearly see the centuries of Roman civilization: here a course of bricks; below it a black streak that indicated a fire or some other disaster, and so on in a *millefeuille* of history. And beneath her feet was a bright yellow mud of prehistory, from the time when there was nothing walking in the Forum but wolves and deer.

The brown mud she was sponging was from the eighth century BC. Romulus is meant to have founded Rome in 753 BC. Could Carandini be right? I don't see why not; and even if Romulus never existed, says the professor, he was of huge mythical importance to Rome.

Never forget, Mr Johnson, he said, that after Rome was founded on 21 April 753 BC there was something very particular about Romulus' approach to government. Rome was not just a place for the indigenous people of this spot. It wasn't defined by its geographical location. He spread the word that the new city was a place of asylum for anyone who wanted a new life.

'Give me your poor, your tired, your huddled masses,' said Romulus, or words to that effect; and there came to Rome exiles, refugees, murderers, criminals and runaway slaves. From the very beginning, therefore, Rome was not defined ethnically; Rome was not defined geographically; Rome was an idea.

In that key respect Roman civilization was very different from Greek civilization. The Greeks divided people into

Greeks and barbarians, where Greekness was as much a matter of blood as of language. For the Romans, bloodlines were irrelevant. They believed that anyone could be a Roman citizen, if he walked the walk and talked the talk. They believed that the highest honour a Roman could be paid was to go down in history as a man who expanded the Roman Empire; and they believed there was no finer destiny for the rest of the world than to be conquered by Rome.

Pliny, the Roman polymath, raves about 'the immeasurable majesty of the Roman peace', and prays that this gift of the gods will last forever. The Romans, he says, have been bestowed upon the rest of the human race like a second source of light.

The interesting thing is how readily the people of the conquered provinces agreed. They did indeed want to be citizens of Rome. They turned their smiling faces towards this second source of light, and basked in its radiance.

If you wander through the museums of Europe you will find touching stone tributes by people who are in the very process of shrugging off their Celtic, Gallic or Germanic names – and becoming Roman.

Take the amphitheatre in Lyons, built in AD 19 during the reign of Tiberius, and which was to become the scene of terrible massacres of the Christians in AD 177. It was dedicated by a local nob called Caius Julius Rufus, who also built the triumphal arch at Saintes. Now roll that name round your mouth: Caius Julius Rufus. Couldn't be more Roman, could it? But his father was called C. Julius Catuaneunius, and his grandfather C. Julius Agedemopas. His great-grandfather was called Epotsorovidus.

You don't have to be equipped with the Roman equivalent of *Debrett's* to see what is happening here. With every generation that we go backwards we find a name that is slightly less

Roman, and slightly more Celtic, until we get to the magnificent Epotsorovidus, who almost certainly fought against the Romans.

If you are wondering why so many of them are called C. Julius, it is for the same reason that so many black American descendants of slaves are called Johnson in honour of the emancipating President Andrew Johnson. They are proud to bear the name of the man who gave them Roman citizenship, after he had conquered Gaul. It was C. Julius Caesar who clearly gave citizenship to Agedemopas.

And even if they didn't achieve full citizenship, it is almost tear-inducing to see how proud the locals were of beginning to look and sound like Romans. In the museum at Mainz there is a sweet memorial to an old couple called Blussus and Menimane. He was obviously a ship-owner, who died at the ripe old age of seventy-five, and the back of their gravestone is decorated with a typical flat-bottomed Rhine transport. One can imagine that he made a fortune supplying the Roman garrison, and in many ways he is making a terrific effort to look Roman in death.

For a start he has a gravestone. Throughout non-Roman northern Europe it had been the practice to cremate the dead, and the spread of gravestones is a sign of the rapidity of Romanization. Then the inscription is in Latin, and he and his wife and son (or possibly slave) are in the characteristic position of Roman grave-reliefs, she with a little dog and spinning implements on her lap, to show what a good wife she is, and he with a scroll to show he can read.

But they are only half-Roman. Look at the Celtic torc around Menimane's neck; look at Blussus' strange hoodie-style collar. And though the inscription is in Latin, it has been charmingly misspelt. Menimane is described as his *uxsor* – which should be *uxor*, for wife. What kind of a name is

Menimane, anyway? And what kind of a name is Blussus, come to that? A thoroughly Germanic or Celtic name lurking beneath that Roman termination.

Still – look at the name of their son, the one who put up the gravestone. He is called Primus. You don't get more Roman than Primus.

What we have here is the process of Romanization frozen in stone. All the Roman pretensions of the Blussus family are on display, and so are the Celtic origins that will almost certainly vanish in the next generation.

Julius Caesar is thought by some to have killed a million people in the conquest of Gaul, and there must have been terrible bitterness and hatreds. And yet everywhere we look in Gaul and in the Roman Empire we find people falling over themselves to get the coveted *tria nomina* – the three names – of the Roman citizen; and across the empire we see the Roman state welcoming people to the roll of the citizenry, with a diversity and Catholicism that puts most modern Western countries to shame.

There is a huge bronze plaque in the Lyons museum, of a magnificent speech made by the emperor Claudius in AD 48, commending to the senate the idea that senators could be drawn from Gaul. He was attacked by conservatives, who accused him of devaluing the coinage of citizenship. But by the end of the second century half the senate was of provincial origin. The Latin authors Seneca, Lucan and Martial all came from Spain, the first two from Cordoba and Martial from Aragon.

The emperor Diocletian was born in Croatia and Constantine was born in Nis in what is now Serbia, a town distinguished by not much except a tobacco factory that was bombed by NATO in 1998 in an act of extreme political correctness. As for the emperor Septimius Severus, who reigned with some success towards the end of the second century, he not only came from what is now Libya, but if you look at the paintings of him he is clearly African in complexion. That kind of distinction meant nothing to the Romans. He lived an astonishing life, crisscrossing Europe on military campaigns; and such was the unity of the empire that he was able to work his way from North Africa to the centre of power. Not a lot of people know that. He also died in York, like Constantius, father of Constantine. Not a lot of people know that, either.

The Roman Empire was like a gigantic Moulinex, swirling soldiers, traders and adventurers from one end to the other. In the reign of Augustus, 68 per cent of legionaries were of Italian origin. By the end of the second century AD only 2 per cent of the army was of Italian origin.

Of course, there were huge divisions in Roman society, and the fate of slaves was grim. But then you always had the possibility of achieving your emancipation, and working your way up; and if society was stratified horizontally, it was not vertically segregated.

The principle established by Romulus held good. Rome was there for everyone who qualified for citizenship. It was a bit like America, in the sense that it didn't matter what your religion was, or where your parents came from, or what your colour was. All that mattered was that you were prepared to buy into the idea of Rome, to show loyalty to the imperial cult, and you were in. People would work their fingers to the bone to become rich enough to be favoured with citizenship; they would become auxiliary soldiers, happily serve twenty-five years in the army, posted to some hell-hole like Carlisle, so that they could obtain citizenship on being demobbed, marry their common-law wives (marriage was forbidden to legionaries until their term of service was over) and then pass citizenship on to their children.

What did they get out of it? Well, again, it was like American citizenship, in that they had the right to vote and to enter into contracts. They could stand for office, and begin to dignify the family name. They had the right not to be beaten in an arbitrary fashion, as we see in the case of Paul. They had a right not to be crucified (Paul was beheaded; Peter, not a Roman citizen, died on the cross).When a Roman citizen faced punishment, the sentence was generally commuted.

But in a way all these advantages are trivial next to the fundamental fact that they were in. They were Roman.

In that sense Roman citizenship was very different from the European 'citizenship' that we all have by virtue of the Treaty of Maastricht. Roman citizenship gave you, the citizen, a specific and unmediated relationship with the emperor. You did not have your citizenship by dint of your membership of some group or nation – as we possess 'European citizenship'. You had it in your own right.

And yet there is still something remarkable about the zeal with which men like Blussus and Agedemopas converted to Rome. Did they have no pride in their own pre-existing culture and civilization?

We have seen from the story of Arminius and Flavus that some of these tribesmen were Romano-sceptics, and some were Romano-philes. What was it about the Roman brand that was so repellent to some and so irresistible to others?

The process of Romanization has been compared to a great tide coming in over a variegated shoreline, so that the beaches and rock pools and seaweed and shingle are all simultaneously obliterated. And what happened hundreds of years later, with the retreat of Rome, was the exposure of those same different formations again – much changed and eroded, of course, but with traces of the original distinctions still apparent.

We need to grope back to the time before the Romans came, and briefly try to understand what kind of a world it was, and why these people so wanted to be Roman. Were they proud to become Roman, or frightened of Roman contempt?

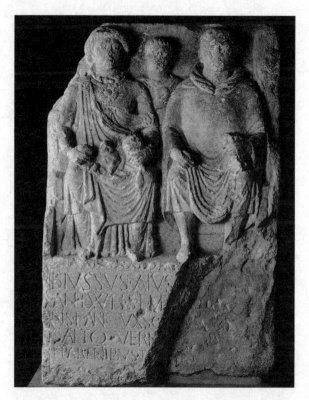

The touching gravestone from Mainz (Moguntiacum) of Blussus, Menimane and their son. It is a portrait of a Celtic family well on the way to becoming Roman.

CHAPTER SIX

The Inheritance from Greece

The library of Celsus, built in what is now Turkey by a Greek-speaking Syrian. But Celsus thought of himself primarily as a Roman.

Like all the best ideas, Roman civilization was really a rip-off of a brilliant idea by someone else. As the Romans had no hesitation in admitting, they owed their inspiration to the Greeks. It was part of Virgil's claim to greatness that he was not only the soi-disant poet of Roman imperialism. His *Aeneid* was also modelled on Homer, the unsurpassed progenitor of the epic. Roman theatre was an imitation of Greek theatre.

Roman philosophy consisted largely of head-gripping discussion of Greek philosophers. Horace was immensely proud of his own literary gifts, but he tells us that it is the summit of his ambition to go down in history as the man who was able to write Greek lyric poetry in Latin.

Posh young Romans would go off to school and universities in Greece – which is where Octavian was when he heard the news of Caesar's death. Indeed, it was expected of all educated Romans that they should speak Greek.

'Did Cicero say anything?' asks Cassius in *Julius Caesar*. 'Ay, he spoke Greek,' says Casca, adding, notoriously, that it was all Greek to him. For once, Shakespeare erred in his feeling for Rome. All the conspirators would have known Greek, Casca included.

Rome was a bilingual empire, and everywhere east of the Adriatic it is probably fair to say that they spoke Greek first, even if official pronouncements were in Latin. When the emperor Claudius is addressed by a barbarian in both Greek and Latin, he says, 'Oh, I see you come armed with both our languages.' It was a society as officially bilingual as modern America, except that in Washington you can still get away without speaking Spanish.

The Romans were acutely conscious of this cultural debt. Horace says, '*Graecia capta ferum victorem cepit et artes intulit agresti Latio.*' 'Captured Greece captured her rough conqueror, and introduced the arts to rustic Latium.'

One can imagine that this idea must have soothed the Greeks, and palliated the indignity of conquest. The Romans were the military masters, but the Greeks were always the ones for culture and brains. Where were the Roman tragedians to match Aeschylus, Sophocles and Euripides? Where were the sculptors to match Myron or Polycleitus? Where were the philosophers to match Plato and Aristotle?

That Augustan architectural style that Augustus spread around the empire like a brand: where did he get it? It was a flagrant pinch from the world's first Corinthian column, which is to be found in the fifth-century temple of Apollo at Bassae in central Greece.

As they beheld the terrifying energy of Rome, spreading and conquering and Romanizing, the Greeks could plausibly console themselves with the thought that this was really a projection and magnification of their own achievement. And that may partly explain the amazing ease with which the Romans took over and governed the Greek city-states. These Greek societies were used to being run by one foreign dynasty or another, Macedonians or Seleucids or whoever. They were used to treating their rulers as gods.

The Greeks pioneered the concept of the city, and the assembly of the citizens, and the agora, the public space that the Romans called the Forum. They gave the Romans the idea of the pantheon of gods, and the theatre, and a million other beautiful inheritances.

But the Greeks were smart enough to be interested in Roman improvements, such as the baths, and the latrines. And arches! These boys could do arches. The Periclean Acropolis is perhaps the single finest and most influential architectural monument in the world. But, gifted though Pericles' team was, none of those Athenian craftsmen had the faintest idea how to make an arch.

So when you go to a place like Ephesus, a city of about 20,000 when Augustus made it the capital of the Roman province of Asia, you see a Roman city somehow growing organically out of Greek civilization. It is like one of those miracle citrus trees that manages to produce oranges and lemons at the same time. It's trabeate and arcuate at once. They do beams, they do arches, they do Greek, they do Latin.

I went to Ephesus before dawn, to miss the crowds, and we were standing there in the chilly twilight when a colleague started to make a noise of approval. 'It's the old currant bun,' he said.

The sun was coming up behind the hill, and the architraves of the top storey were turning dull pink, and then rose, and then gold, as the morning light washed down over a building that in so many ways symbolizes the triumph of Graeco-Roman civilization.

'You look at that building,' he said, 'and you think, really, it's been downhill ever since.' And one can see what he means. It is hard to think of any Renaissance or Baroque building that matches it for confidence, grandeur or simplicity. As for the classicizing pastiches of Quinlan Terry, it's like comparing a five-year-old's drawing of mum to the *Mona Lisa*.

There are four aediculae, or two-column porticoes, that protrude on the ground floor, and there are three entrances between the aediculae, and in the walls of the aediculae are niches in which there were statues of Sophia, Episteme, Eunoia and Arete – Greek embodiments of the wisdom, knowledge, goodwill and virtue of the man who endowed it.

But the really cunning feature is the way the three aediculae of the upper level are built to span the gaps between those of the lower level, so as to create a two-storey portico over the entrance. It's like a trick picture by Escher, in which the gap between the porticoes becomes the portico itself; and it absorbs the eye. And if you still can't visualize it, just look at the side of a London bus, because the library of Celsus is rightly used by the Turks as an example of the finest tourist attraction in modern Turkey.

Inside this building were 12,000 scrolls and, again, they would have been both Greek and Latin, Homer as well as Virgil. It was built in AD 117 by Tiberius Julius Celsus Polemeanus, and the notable thing about Celsus was that he came from Syria. He probably grew up speaking some Middle Eastern dialect, with Greek as his principal language.

Not only are the inscriptions on the building in Greek, but Celsus' son caused the creation of a statue outside it, in honour of the wisdom of his father, labelled, in Greek, '*Sophia Kelsou*' – the genius of Celsus. And yet how did he think of himself?

He was a Roman, and a Roman proconsul at that. As we all goggled at these old stones warming and blushing in the sun, I thought of that library as a symbol of the amazing Greek readiness to adapt and fuse.

There is a famous story in the Bible of how Paul came to Ephesus, and a man called Demetrios became alarmed by this account of a new monotheistic Hebrew-derived religion. He was the president of the guild of Ephesian silversmiths, and they made their money by knocking up silver images of the local goddess, Diana, and flogging them to tourists. In fact, the goddess was originally the Greek goddess Artemis, whom the Romans identified with Diana, but what the hell, said the Greeks. They were the same, really. They were both virgins, and they could both be depicted with the same jolly cascade of bosoms running down their fronts, and turned into something that was, and still is, a highly sellable knick-knack.

This Jesus business, on the other hand, appeared to be a potential blight on trade. Paul was converting the people of Ephesus to Christianity, and the Christians had a down on other cults. So Demetrios got a great claque of his fellow silversmiths and rip-off merchants into the theatre, and for hours on end they shouted 'Great is Diana of the Ephesians!' It is a testament to Greek suppleness that when this show of commercially inspired devotion failed, and Christianity kept gaining ground, they tried another tack. They started to

119

consider the possibilities of this here Mary, mother of God.

She was certainly a virgin. She was famous for her breasts (so to speak), even if they were not as numerous as Diana's. It was not long before Ephesus was full of mumbo-jumbo about how it was the final resting place of the Virgin Mary, and the heirs of Demetrios are to this day selling statues not just of Diana/Artemis, but of Mary as well.

If you walk around Ephesus, down its magnificent shopping streets, past its baths and brothels and theatres, you can understand how the Roman empire worked so well in the east of the Mediterranean, and how it came to last so much longer than in the west. The Romans were going with the grain when they conquered Greece. They arrived in a world that was already politically sophisticated, highly literate, and urbane in both senses: it was a world of cities.

They took these Greek institutions, tweaked them, adapted them, and rolled them out through western Europe as well. And that was the hard bit; because it was there that they found people who had never lived in cities, who had no idea about baths, and who had neither knowledge of nor interest in philosophical concepts.

They were the pre-existing tribes of France, Germany, Spain, Portugal, Belgium, Britain, Holland, Switzerland, Austria, Hungary, the Czech Republic and other members of the current EU. They were, by the standards of Graeco-Roman culture, complete barbarians.

No doubt that is now in some sense politically incorrect. I imagine that you can find academics who will tell you that their culture was just as high and noble as that of the invaders; that their lumpy sculptures are no whit inferior to Roman statuary, and that if only we could make it out, their runic scratching masks a literary art as fine as Homer or Virgil.

I had a wonderful conversation with M. Jacques Lasfargues, the keeper of antiquities at the Museum of Lyons. He has a peerless collection of Gallo-Roman exhibits, but such is his political psychology that he cannot help identifying the Romans with the Americans.

Their culture spread everywhere, he kept telling me gloomily. It was like Coca-Cola. It was like Hollywood. Throughout our conversation, therefore, he kept trying to persuade me of the wonders of the various Celtic bits and bobs in his custody, a bronze wine sieve, for instance, that proves that the pre-Roman Gauls drank and greatly appreciated wine; the extraordinary skill with which the Celts had made a bronze wagon, each wheel cast by *cire perdue* (lost wax), as long ago as the eighth century BC – while Romulus was still being suckled by a she-wolf.

I am afraid I wasn't quite convinced by his philo-Celticism, and nor were the Latin writers. The further you went, the more barbaric it becomes. Tacitus writes contemptuously of the lifestyle of the Fenni, a northern tribe identified with the Finns, who live in grotesque poverty. He tells us that they have no weapons, no horses, no homes. They feed on herbs, dress in skins, and have earth for a bed. They tip their arrows with bone because they have no metal. The women go out hunting with the men, and take their share of the spoils. The whole thing is hopelessly uncouth.

As for the non-Roman tribes nearer the empire, they hardly get a better press. We have discussed Tacitus on the Germans, their hysterical mood swings, their sad, desolate country, bristling with forests or foul with marshes, their runty cattle, their appalling barley-induced hangovers.

When Augustus is explaining why he is not going to bother to conquer Britain, he says that the country supplies nothing but dogs, and isn't worth the cost of a garrison. And anyway, all Romans knew that the British drank milk! Disgusting.

Such are the barbaro-phobic stereotypes of the Romans, and the barbarians – and we, their descendants – cannot answer back. They had no literature; they had no history; they had very little by way of the plastic or graphic arts. All we know is that they fought the Romans for centuries before they finally gave in.

It took 200 years before the Romans subdued the Celtiberians and Turdetanians of Spain, and still there were important pockets of resistance, like the Pyrenees, where they speak Basque to this day as a reminder of their refusal to surrender to the Latin-speaking armies. The Spanish still use the Celtic word – *cerveza* – for beer. Julius Caesar seriously exaggerates the success of his operation in Gaul, and fighting continued well into the reign of Augustus. As for Germany, we know all about Varus and Arminius.

We know what these people were fighting against – the Roman legions, which were impelled across Europe by the Roman aristocracy's competitive love of conquest.

It is less clear what they were fighting for. Nowadays it is held to be incorrect to think in terms of any spirit of pre-Roman nationhood, or nationalism. When Tacitus calls Arminius the 'liberator of Germany', he is supposed to be introducing an anachronism. I am not so sure. The sheer number of revolts must surely have had something to do not just with taxes, but with a deep conservative sense of outrage at what the Romans had done to their traditions and their self-government.

Whatever their motives for resistance, they lost, and under the prevailing theology of the day the fact that they lost showed that it was divinely willed that they should lose.

They lost because the Romans were militarily superior, and once it was clear that the gig was up for the independence of the tribes of northern Europe, the elites in those tribes did what elites have always done. They ratted. They began the glorious process of collaboration.

In Roman sculpture it is always easy to tell the difference between Romans and barbarians. The barbarians have beards, they wear trousers, and they are getting badly beaten.

CHAPTER SEVEN

Winning Over the Elites

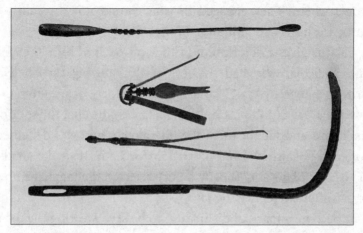

Smooth operators. The Romans were fastidious about body hair, and when they invaded Britain there was a boom in tweezers.

Suppose you were a nob in pre-Roman Spain or France, and you saw the dust of the tramping legions as they approached your higgledy-piggledy fort. What would your feelings be? Apart from the terror of being slaughtered by the world's most vicious killing machine, or being crucified for resistance, what else would you feel?

You're the man with the massy golden Celtic bracelet; you've got the fancy helmet and the cattle and the expensive wife. The

125

reason you are fighting, and the reason you most fear the Romans, is that you think they will mean the end of the established order.

You think the Romans are like everyone else you've been fighting in your brutish existence, and that their main strategic objective is to rape your daughters, slaughter your cattle and drink horrible grain-based potions from your sawn-off skull.

Well, the Romans were smarter than that. They did not kill the elites. With infinite cunning, and with supreme confidence in the product they were selling, they co-opted them. They wooed them. They engaged in what would now be called a battle for hearts and minds, and they won.

Tacitus gives a description of the approach of his father-in-law, Agricola, who had the job of Romanizing the ancient Britons between AD 77 and 84, about forty years after the conquest. He didn't pick on the chiefs; he educated the sons of the chiefs and taught them the liberal arts, and was delighted when the British showed more flair for Latin than the Gauls. 'Those that had only shortly before rejected the language now strove after eloquence,' he says.

It became a mark of distinction to be seen wearing the toga, and gradually, laments the cynical historian, the savage ancient Britons declined into attractive Roman vices. They hobnobbed in porticos; they went to the baths and washed off their woad. It was the beginning of a scourge that has never vanished from these islands – *elegantia conviviorum* – dinner parties.

They called it civilization, he scoffs – *humanitas* – when in reality it was a form of slavery!

Slavery or not, the local toffs couldn't get enough of it.

They changed their styles of pottery, their beliefs about the dead, the way they dealt with the corpses of their loved ones. They started baking bread instead of making porridge, and drinking wine instead of beer, and all the time the Romans had the wit to lead them on, to encourage them, and to keep them in power.

The Romans didn't impose new gods on them; they had a system called *interpretatio*, whereby pagan gods could be fitted into the Roman pantheon. So the Gauls were particularly big on a god called Lug, who was associated with transport and commerce. No problem, said the Romans. Let's say Lug and Mercury are the same. Tremendous, said the Gauls, and in no time they were paying large sums to build temples to Mercury.

The Romans didn't mind which gods they worshipped: the adherence to Taranis, Epona and Sucellus was just as proper as the belief in Mars, Apollo and Minerva. They only stipulated that observance should be made with proper Roman religious sensibility. That meant no animal heads and no human sacrifice; anything else was fine.

It turned out that these chiefs had been wrong to think of the Roman conquest as the end of their authority. They had a new role, as mediators between the tribesmen and the Romans, and they had a new source of political support – the Romans and their legions, and not the fractious common people of Gaul, or Spain, or Germany, or Britain.

In return for helping to organize the taxes, they were given citizenship, and the Romans were careful to leave them with the illusion of self-government. The Romans offered them a new definition of what it meant to be a human being, and across the empire the ruling thugs and villains became converts to this new concept of *humanitas* – the attribute of a civilized man.

And *humanitas*, they learned from their Roman teachers, had several components. These included:

benevolentia	goodwill
observantia	respect
mansuetudo	gentleness

127

facilitas	affability
severitas	austerity
dignitas	merit, reputation
gravitas	authority, weight.

Tremendous, they grunted, chucking their trousers out and tweezering their nose hairs. A spot of the old *dignitas*. That's what we want. And show me some *observantia*, darling, and pass me the mirror.

It was a key part of Roman ideology that their civilization was superior – a second sun for the universe – and that assumption was accepted to a degree that was almost painful. People yearned to be awarded the baubles that were marks of preferment in Rome, just as my in-laws, whiskery Sikhs in the Punjab, were once thrilled to the core to be made knights of the British Empire.

Writing at the end of the first century AD, or the beginning of the second, Plutarch describes the frenzied scrabbling of provincial worthies as they tried to get up the *cursus honorum*, the career ladder. He speaks of the Greek, or the Spaniard, or the Asian, who is not content if he has won the glory or power that goes with a certain position among his fellows. Oh no – he is in tears if he does not wear the shoes of a patrician senator.

And if he does make it to the senate, he blubs because he is not yet a praetor, and if a praetor, he blubs because he wants to be a consul; and if he is elected to the consulship, he snivels because he should have been the first consul to be elected that year, and not the second. And so on.

The genius of this approach, this fostering of Roman ambition in the breasts of these provincials, was that it not only kept them quiet, and kept the old power structures in place. It was also wonderfully cheap.

All the energy that had gone into pointless blood feuds and cattle rustling now became sublimated into Roman-style swanking and glory chasing. In the words of Aelius Aristides 'all the other forms of rivalry have passed away from the cities, and this one form of emulation preoccupies them all: how each one is going to appear as attractive and beautiful as it can. Everywhere is full of training grounds, fountains, imposing gateways, temples, workshops, schools.' The world has been in distress since ancient times, he says, and it has been brought back to health.

In other words the Romans were able to use the competitive spirit of these newly Romanizing provincials to build great works – and not a penny, of course, had to come from imperial funds. When we look around Europe, at the massive legacy of Roman masonry that can still be seen striding across our fields, we shouldn't kid ourselves that these were projects paid for by Romans. They were far too fly for that.

These *grands projets* were sometimes paid for by the taxes of the provincials, but more often by private individuals, and generated by their raw unbridled snobbery.

Sometimes in their lust for Roman distinction the provincials could become embarrassingly vulgar. One of the advantages of being a citizen was that you could hold office in the priesthood of Augustus, which was a form of local government. But like everything else in Rome, it was competitive. You needed to be elected to the *seviri*, and some Gallic chiefs were so keen to suck up to the electorate that they threw games of ever greater lavishness, until Tiberius had to intervene to restrain them.

Think of the psychological brilliance of that idea – wrapping the priesthood of Augustus and local government into one.

The higher the office you seek for yourself, the greater the devotion you must show – *ex officio* – to the emperor and to Rome.

And now let us consider, as we must, what the European Union offers by way of inducements to the elites of Europe. What prizes are there for the elites of the EU, what encouragements to become more 'European'? As it happens, they are not negligible.

Go into Club Class on any flight between European capitals and the chances must be quite high that you will find someone whose ticket has been paid for, one way or the other, by the EU. He or she will be going to some fine hotel in some attractive destination, for an important conference on social exclusion or the greenhouse effect or sexual harassment in the workplace. He or she will have a fantastic time, attended by every comfort, serenaded by the local string quartet and entertained by gorgeous pouting interpreters. And at the end of it one would expect him or her to be invisibly knitted closer to the idea of a united Europe, wouldn't one?

But if the elites of Europe are traditionally in favour of integration, and more Club Class flights, something seems to inhibit them from campaigning more vociferously, and here we must accept a key difference between Europe ancient and modern.

The elites of Europe are far more tightly and viciously accountable to the electorates than the leading lights of the provincial Roman Empire. In modern Europe it would be fair to say that the electorate as a whole is more Euro-sceptic than the elite, and the modern European elite cannot go too far ahead of popular opinion.

But it is very hard to know what the masses really thought of Rome in the provincial Roman Empire. According to Professor Greg Woolf of St Andrews University only 10 per cent of the population of the Gallic provinces lived in the city, and only 6.5 per cent of the population of Britain. He says that you could live your whole life, as a shepherd, or swineherd, or wood-cutter, in some parts of Gaul, and not have any real understanding that you were living in the Roman Empire at all.

For your average swineherd in Gaul, therefore, the Roman Empire was not so much a threat to ancient freedoms, it was just another way by which the same old elites consolidated their privileges.

For the elites – and not just for the elites – it might be a kind of slavery, as Tacitus describes it. But if they had lost their freedom, the provinces had found an increasingly gilded cage.

CHAPTER EIGHT

The Roman Economic Community:
Pax Means Tax

Provence was so peaceful that people could go their lives without seeing a soldier. The point of this triumphal arch at Orange was to remind people how that peace was created.

On the outskirts of Orange is a drab sort of roundabout, with a solitary hotdog stand intended, perhaps, for lorry drivers. In the middle of the reservation is an arch, much blackened by fumes.

133

The sulphur has eaten away at the stone faces of the sculptures, and much of the relief-work has fallen away. We aren't even sure when in the first century AD it was erected, or even who erected it. We aren't sure which battle, if any, it is meant to be commemorating.

But even after two millennia the message of the Roman triumphal arch at Orange is blindingly obvious. First of all, what is an arch? Why did the Romans build these curious freestanding structures as emblems of victory?

An arch is like a gigantic fortified gateway, except that there are no walls on either side. There are no walls on either side because the place is at peace, and the arch is the symbol of that peace.

Orange is the old Roman Arausio, in the middle of Provence. By the first century ad southern Gaul had become so peaceful that Pliny says it is more like Italy than a province. The people of Provence could go about their lives and hardly ever see a soldier. They could get on with getting and spending and becoming more Roman, and never have to think about the sacrifices that made their lives possible.

And that is the point of the Arch of Triumph. High on the front of it we see scenes of battle, barbarians being trampled under the hooves of Roman horses; barbarians being skewered.

This arch is a propagandizing reminder to the population of the basic equations of the Roman Empire. This thing they enjoy called peace did not come about by accident. It was the result of extreme violence by the Roman army. In fact, the Latin word *pax* does not quite mean peace in the sense of the absence of war. It means peace as the result of war. *Pax* means violent pacification. The arch is saying to the passer-by, there is no peace without war, and no war without the army.

Here is Tacitus' account of the Roman governor of Gaul,

Petilius Cerealis, explaining the facts of life to some rebellious Gauls in about AD 69.

Look here, he says: there were always rival kingdoms and wars among the Gauls, before the Romans came. We imposed the *Pax Romana*, and we needed just one thing to do so. 'For there cannot be peace among the peoples without armies, nor armies without pay, nor pay without taxes,' he says. That's the deal, he says, so don't be silly. If the Romans were to depart, then the Gauls would just end up fighting among themselves. Learn the lessons of history, he says: resistance leads to ruin, obedience leads to security.

The paradox of the triumphal arch was that it was even more necessary in times of peace. Why are we paying all these taxes, people must have wondered. Why are we kowtowing to these grasping Roman taxmen? The arch supplied the answer. The army created that peace; that peace was always vulnerable, as the terrible news from Germany testified in AD 9; indeed, there are some who think that it suited the Roman regime to exaggerate the scale of the Varus disaster for precisely the same propaganda purpose – to underline the fragility of peace. It doesn't matter. The message was the same, however many legions Varus lost: the price of *pax* was tax.

It was a price worth paying, because the result of peace was trade, and growing prosperity.

Imperial Rome was the biggest city the world had ever seen. Her population is estimated to have been a million souls, more than any other city until eighteenth-century London. Many of them lived in great squalor, and died so prematurely that there was an annual net inwards migration of 15,000 people. They died in fires in their *insulae*, or apartments; they died of disease. According to Tacitus, 10,000 people perished when a rickety wooden stadium collapsed, which puts some of our modern disasters into perspective. Was there an inquiry? Was there a minute's silence? Did people go around wearing special ribbons in memory of the great rickety stadium disaster? Did they hell.

Rome got on with it, a giant beating pulse at the centre of her Mediterranean empire. If you go down to the old port of Ostia, and you look at the immense granaries where the corn was unloaded from Egypt, Tunisia and Sicily, you have an idea of the scale of her needs. You can see what the author of the Book of Revelation meant when he referred to the imperial city as the Whore of Babylon. He talks of the trade in 'gold, silver, jewels and pearls, fine linen, purple, silk and scarlet, all kinds of scented wood, all articles of ivory, all articles of costly wood, bronze, iron and marble, cinnamon, spice, incense, myrrh, frankincense, wine, olive oil, choice flour and wheat, cattle and sheep, horses and chariots, slaves and human lives'. He was right. Rome was a magnetic orifice, and the exorbitant prices she would pay pulled in goods from all over the world. (It was not until 1850 that another hippopotamus was seen in Western Europe.) It all came through Ostia, was unloaded by a slave population estimated at 17,000, put on barges and taken up the Tiber to Rome.

Sometimes the number of grain vessels was so great that the harbour would get jammed, and Trajan built a magnificent hexagonal port so that they would have more room to unload. You can still see that port, and you can imagine the stevedores unloading Rome's 100,000 tonnes of grain per year; but do not believe for one minute that this was the simple operation of supply and demand.

The grain market in ancient Rome was as rigged as anything in the Common Agricultural Policy; and in the obsession with price-fixing, the massive subsidies, you might even say that the modern EU is imitating her ancient avatar. The

CAP was in theory called into being so that the population of Europe should never again experience shortage of food; and that was exactly the prospect that terrified the emperors.

If the mob got hungry, the mob would get angry. That is why the Roman state had, in 123 BC, instituted a corn dole. You had a ticket, which you could present to the corn dole office, and if you were one of 200,000–250,000 eligible adult males you would get 33 kilos of wheat per month, which was more than enough for an adult, though not enough for a family. In due course it was more than just a corn dole: there were state hand-outs of wine and pork and even olive oil.

Nor was it means-tested. In the second century BC the great social reformer Gaius Gracchus was standing proudly watching the corn dole queue when he saw a famous aristocrat in line. 'Oi,' said the champion of the poor, 'what are you doing here?'

'Well,' said the toff (who rejoiced in the toff-ish name of L. Calpurnius Piso Frugi, ex-consul), 'I disapprove of you giving out my property to every Tom, Dick or Harry, but since you are going to give it out, I am going to have my share, too.' Thus speak all the nobility of Oxfordshire, in deciding whether or not they are morally entitled to use the bus tokens intended for the poorest pensioners of the county. I've jolly well paid my stamp, they say, and I want the benefit.

The corn dole required immense organization. There was the *praefectus annonae*, and the *procurator annonae*, the first being based in Rome and the second in Ostia, and desperate efforts were made to control the prices – just as the modern EU officials are engaged in perpetual and doomed struggles with the boys on the grain futures markets. Private traders would exploit the position, so that wheat prices in Rome were four times higher than those in Egypt. The total cost of supplying the city with grain was about 15 per cent of the state's revenues. The emperors had no choice but to keep the grain coming.

137

Once when there was a shortage the emperor Claudius found himself being pelted with bread rolls as he walked down the street, and had to flee. He immediately offered Roman citizenship to anyone who would commission a grain ship capable of carrying 10,000 *modii*, or 20,000 gallons of wheat – a supertanker.

Much later the emperor Domitian was so alarmed by the shortage of domestically grown wheat that he ordered all the vineyards of Provence to be grubbed up – one of the first examples of the kind of agricultural intervention that has been commonplace in Europe over the last fifty years. He only relented when he was lobbied by the Gallo-Roman wine producers – one of the first examples of successful lobbying.

And the big controversies of Roman agriculture were remarkably similar to those we have today. The Romans had *latifundia* – big prairie farms, operated by chain gangs of miserable slaves, and the Latin poets are full of longing for the days before the clearances, when each man tilled his own row of beans.

In reality these Latin poets lived in the cities among multitudes who benefited from subsidized food. When they bewailed the loss of the old ways, they were about as consistent as the politicians and journalists of today's Britain, who lambast Tesco for forcing down the prices paid to farmers and then whip round it in half an hour on a Saturday when they do their weekly shopping.

Nor was grain the only market in which the politicians interfered. They had to keep up the supply of olive oil, a commodity to which the Romans attributed semi-miraculous properties and efficacy. They used it for cooking, they used it for lighting, they used it for shampoo and for soap, and when they got to the dregs of the amphora they scooped it out and used its spermicidal qualities as a contraceptive.

Of all the ruins I have seen in Rome, perhaps the most bizarre is called Monte Testaccio, a gigantic rubbish dump, taller than the tallest building in the Forum. You go through an old wrought-iron gate, and you walk up a strange overgrown path, and if you look more closely at the ground beneath you see that it is made up of terracotta clinker, endless fragments of thick red clay potsherd. It is 20,000 metres square, and the hill contains 25 million amphorae, taken and smashed by the ancient municipal authorities. Almost all of them – 83 per cent – were Spanish olive oil containers from Baetica, and they were smashed by the state because something nasty happens to olive oil amphorae when they have been allowed to hold the stuff for too long, and the properties of the gunk become not just spermicidal but probably homicidal as well.

So the Romans had a state-funded amphorae-smashing operation. The bureaucrats intervened in the price of olive oil, going out to Spain to tell the growers how much would be needed. They used huge quantities of taxpayers' money in the grain market, and regarded grain supply as a key political question.

How, you may wonder, can I possibly extol the Roman system as a free market? It sounds positively Stalinist, put like that. And yet the reality is that agriculture – and the economy in general – were far freer in ancient Rome than they are in modern Europe.

They had no welfare state to speak of, apart from the various doles, and a modest scheme started by Trajan called the *alimenta*, by which the state subsidized agricultural mortgages and the mortgage payments were used in turn to pay for a kind of child benefit for the middle classes. They had no state health service, and about half government spending went on the army. And even the Roman army was comparatively small, and amazingly efficient.

The Romans ran their empire of 80–100 million people with an army of about 300,000–400,000, half of them legionaries and half of them auxiliaries. In other words, the military presence consisted of only about 2 per cent of the adult male population.

How does a modern government mainly spend our taxes? About 85–90 per cent of it goes on the salaries of public officials, who make up about 30 per cent of the working population; and the miracle of Rome was that, by comparison with ourselves, they ran this enormous territory with a microscopic bureaucracy.

They were certainly ruthless in collecting taxes, and had no scruples about entrusting the operation to some pretty corrupt people. The emperor Vespasian called them his 'sponges', because first they soaked up the money from the provincials and then he had the pleasure of prosecuting them, and squeezing out the sponges. But they had a tiny staff for the imperial revenue collection – perhaps one man for every 400,000 people.

As for the total tax take, it is estimated by the late Keith Hopkins to have been between 10 and 5 per cent – perhaps less – of gross domestic product; and that compares with the 40p in every pound that the British government takes today.

The emperors had no economic policy as we would understand it today. They had no medium-term financial strategy. Come to that, they had no long- or short-term financial strategy, either. They did not borrow to pay for the activities of the state, nor did they play any particular role in setting interest rates – though their activities could have an effect on the price of money. Gold prices tumbled when Julius Caesar returned from Gaul, laden with bullion, and when Augustus had defeated Antony and Cleopatra he brought back so much treasure from Egypt that interest rates fell by 60 per cent.

But it was all unplanned and unscripted. The emperor's economic objectives were few and simple: to keep the corn dole coming, to pay for the circuses, and above all to pay for the army. He didn't much care which fund the cash came from. In theory there was meant to be a clear division between the patrimonium, or estates, of the emperor, and the state treasuries. In reality, the emperor was able to write cheques on both accounts, and most were far from scrupulous about making the distinction. They would use the same funds to pay for their jesters as to pay for the troops shivering on Hadrian's Wall; and no one objected, because to the Roman way of thinking it was obvious that the emperor *was* the state.

Nor were they scrupulous in their cash-raising methods. From the very beginning, when Augustus expropriated the assets of his murdered enemies, they had used a system called *bona damnatorum* – condemning men to death and swiping the proceeds. It came to Nero's notice that six men owned half of the Roman province of Africa – so he had them bumped off and became the proprietor himself. Caligula persecuted some affluent Gallic nobles, and took 600 million sesterces. Claudius executed thirty-five senators and 300 knights, and is thought to have made a pretty penny out of the operation.

Under the reign of the flagrantly evil Domitian there was a cash crunch caused by his decision to increase soldiers' pay at the same time as a lavish scheme of entertainment and building. He financed this with a horrible programme of extortion, in which anyone might be accused of *lèse-majesté* towards the emperor before being executed and despoiled. Soon there was a financial incentive to betray any anti-imperial 'indiscretions' to the authorities, and Rome acquired a nightmarish culture of *delatores* – sneaks – as creepy as anything in Ceauçescu's Romania.

If all else failed, they would melt down the statues of their predecessors, or put a tax on the urinals, or sell off the palace dwarves; and when the empire turned Christian, the emperors had the perfect excuse to seize the treasures of the pagan temples and sell them off, too.

At the heart of Roman economics – if that is not an oxymoron – there was one key question: how big should the empire be? In one sense, the bigger the better. The more people Rome controlled, the more tax the emperor was able to exact. Between 225 and 25 BC the numbers of people under Roman rule rose from 4 million to 60 million. But the increase in revenues was proportionally much greater, increasing about a hundredfold, mainly because Rome was then absorbing the rich mini-empires of Macedonia, Egypt and Syria.

And yet it was obvious that this policy of expansion was not always financially sensible. There were the great tracts of northern Europe where the Romans never ventured, not because they were militarily incapable, but because it was not worth it. The settlements were too sparse, the land too poor. The more dangerous and difficult the territories the empire engulfed, the more expensive it was to control them. That meant stationing more troops on the frontier. Which meant paying the troops more, at a time when no extra tax revenues were coming in.

Even the Romans, with their GCSE economics, understood that if you wanted to increase public expenditure on the army, and you couldn't find the extra money in tax, then the inevitable result was inflation. In the end it was that inflation, and the attendant economic insecurity, that was to be among the causes of the collapse.

For all the eccentricity of their tax-raising methods and the oddness of their spending priorities, the Roman emperors produced some fantastic economic results. For about a 100 years they managed to keep public-sector wage inflation running at zero – in the sense that a legionary's annual pay remained fixed at 900 sesterces. During the period of the *Pax Romana* we have hardly any evidence of inflation in the west of the empire, and in the east it seems to have been running at about 0.85 per cent.

Roman Europe was largely a pre-industrial society, in which wealth was locked up in land and labour; and yet the Roman peace was so perfect and so tranquil that many people became quite shockingly rich. If you go to Trier in Germany, you can see the funerary monuments of the wine tycoons, made in about AD 200. They are huge stone sculptures of boats, childish in their simplicity and enthusiasm, in which the deceased are depicted rowing enormous cargoes of wine barrels up the Moselle. There are reliefs of the deceased sitting at a table while servants come up and tip out sackfuls of coin.

It is all hilariously vulgar, and reminiscent of the funerary monument of Trimalchio, the fictional millionaire in Petronius. He imagines himself beautifully carved with all the trimmings – pet dog, ships in sail, you name it. He is sitting in his magistrate's seat in a purple-bordered toga wearing five gold rings and scattering coins to the people from a bag. If you are momentarily taken aback by the idea of purple and gold on a funeral monument, remember that these things were painted. When we look at carvings from the ancient world, we forget that they were as gloriously slathered in make-up as an ageing film star. They were inexpressibly gaudy.

There is something sweet and innocent and utterly pre-Christian in this celebration of life and death in Roman Germany. It is all about the joy of making wine, and the joy of making money, and the slow and irresistible plopping of oars as this delicious white Moselle was carried up the river to the North Sea, and Britain, or down it to hook up with the Rhône, and thence to Marseilles and the Mediterranean. There was no extra moral virtue that they wished to celebrate. Wine-making was the virtue, and their success was blessed by the gods.

These stately aquatic journeys were possible because the Roman army had cleared the river of pirates. The *Pax Romana* provided security, the first essential condition for capitalism and investment. It also provided a legal framework, the Roman law that is among the greatest bequests from that day to this.

The fifth-century Roman historian Priscus describes a conversation he had with a merchant who had fought for the barbarian Huns. They argue the advantages of Roman and Hunnic societies; then Priscus plays his ace. He points out that there are many ways of giving freedom, and that the advantage of Roman society is that the dead can bestow their estates as they wish, and that whatever a man has willed for his estates at his death is legally binding. At which point the Roman-turned-Hun weeps and says that the laws are just and Roman polity is good.

He was right, that old Hun. The Romans provided peace, and security of title, and a huge and settled territory with decent transport links. In the very act of levying taxes they actually encouraged economic activity, as people scampered that little bit faster to meet their extra obligations. As the legionaries' pay entered the system, Iron Age barter economies became monetized, and with money came the division of labour.

When the Romans came to northern and western Europe, they found a primitive society based on subsistence agriculture and plunder. With the introduction of Romanized towns, and market day, there came the notion of selling off your surplus, and profits.

The Romans, in other words, produced the first essay in a European Common Market. It was hugely successful, and they did it with far less fuss, and far less regulation, than the equivalent system today.

Much of the trade remained 'cellular'; that is, local to the town or garrison of the area. But some products and merchants travelled immense distances; and what is so instructive about the Roman experience is that they did not bother to harmonize or standardize the products that came on the market.

They left the market alone, and they found that harmonization took place naturally, as the population of Europe succumbed to the lunar pull of the Roman example. If you want an idea of how free trade can produce uniformity of taste, consider the case of *garum*, the notorious Roman fish sauce.

Wine tycoons from Trier. The Moselle was peaceful and lush. The climate was perfect for grapes. It seemed the *Pax Romana* would last forever.

CHAPTER NINE

The Approximation of Taste

The Romans had a big thing about fish, and they fetched enormous prices. In 92 BC a censor – a top official – wept for the death of his favourite lamprey, and said it was as if he had lost a daughter. They also loved fish sauce.

No one knows the exact recipe for *garum*, but it is thought to have been made roughly as follows. You took the blood and viscera of salted fish, together with small whole fish such as anchovies, and you put the mixture in a brine solution and left it in the sun for two months. Or, if you wanted your *garum* more quickly, you could leave it in a heated room. The results were phenomenal.

If you wanted your fish sauce to be slightly less malodorous, you could continue to boil up the gunge for a further four hours, until you had a clear fluid the Romans called *liquamen*.

I know of only one British academic who has tried to make *garum*: Clive Bridger, the keeper of antiquities at Xanten in Germany. In their quiet village house near the Rhine, Clive and his wife Kersten offered me a Roman meal that was historically accurate in almost every respect.

We had a delicious kind of ricotta starter called *moretum*, and lamb with apricots, and *dulcia* – Roman sweets – to follow that are a bit like Turkish baklava. We drank warm wine with nutmeg flour. Everything, I felt, was just as it might have been eaten by Augustus. Except for the fish sauce.

The fish sauce was from Indonesia, and it was from a bottle. What? I asked, no proper *garum*?

'The last time I made *garum*,' said Clive, 'was at university. I did it in a rubbish bin. It was a disaster. I made the whole house completely uninhabitable.'

Like the art of marble sculpture, it would seem that the Roman knack of making *garum* has been lost to posterity. All we know is that they made it on an industrial scale, and loved it with a passion that seems slightly sinister.

The earliest mention of Spanish *garum* is in the fifth century BC. As the Roman Empire grew mighty, it seems to have grown mighty on *garum*. They marinated their meat in it; they put it on their porridge; they used it on almost everything, and because it was so versatile it was also expensive – 1,000 sesterces for about twelve pints.

We have found great factories on the coasts of Spain and Portugal, waterproofed concrete vats in which were still visible the decomposed remnants of tuna fish. We know of other big *garum* plants on the African coast, where bubbling asphaltic pools of fish gut fermented in the sun, decanted and reheated until the liquid was of radioactive potency.

But the remarkable thing about *garum*, for our present purposes, was its ubiquity. Spanish *garum* amphorae have been found at Colchester, at Verulamium (St Albans) and at Hadrian's Wall, and they normally make up about 10 per cent of the total amphora population.

If you dive below the surface of the Mediterranean and find a Roman wreck, there is a high chance that you will find a cargo of *garum*; and if you find a Spanish vessel, about 60 per cent of its load will typically be *garum* or *liquamen*.

The *garum* habit gripped the Romans for centuries, and only seems to have died out with the coming of the Christians, who disapproved of spiciness as much as they disapproved of the immodesty of the baths. Until then the *garum* lust was spread over the Roman world, as uniformly as the sauce itself might be spread over a dry old legionary's biscuit.

We find *garum* amphorae all over Italy, and in France, and Spain and Portugal and North Africa. They used *garum* in Nijmegen, in Palestine, in Bulgaria and in Switzerland.

What does this teach us, given that *garum* was probably if not disgusting at least an acquired taste? It shows the phenomenal conforming influence of Roman cultural preferences on the world they conquered. Across the Roman world, people were becoming conditioned not just to want Roman citizenship, but to adore the same foul-smelling fish mulch that the Romans put on their food.

If we now drag our eyes back from Rome and look at modern Europe, we can see how different we are. We are still deeply sequestrated in our sauces. The Belgians put mayonnaise on their chips – in a way that many British people find shocking – and are themselves appalled to find that we sprinkle our chips with vinegar. The Germans would not dream of putting English mustard on their frankfurters. The French would be quite disgusted if you offered them Marmite or Vegemite, and the Italians know nothing of brown sauce.

But in the Roman world it was *garum, garum, garum*. It was a kind of Euro-ketchup. It was as if you could go to any hotel from Portugal to Iraq, from Scotland to Libya, and expect to find Worcestershire Sauce on the dining-room table.

The *garum* phenomenon is a perfect illustration of the Roman way of creating this elusive sense of identity. It is harmonization without regulation. The conquered people were not forced to eat *garum*; of course not. But *garum* was a distinguishing feature of Roman life.

And if you wanted to show that you were becoming Roman, you pinched your nose, opened the amphora and glooped it all over.

It was peace, and trade, and the slow crawling motion of human beings across the quiet map of Europe. These were the causes of the *garum* phenomenon, and of the universal use of *terra sigillata*, the embossed red Roman Euro-crockery that crops up all over the empire.

Travel was slow and a horse was still the fastest vehicle on earth. Even in times of real emergency, such as the troop revolt on the Rhine in AD 69, it took nine days to bring the news from Moguntiacum (Mainz) to Rome.

But the risks of travelling were diminishing and the incentives increasing. In the first century AD we find a sharp increase in shipwrecks, not because the sea was getting any rougher, but because more ships were putting out into the Mediterranean, the internal sea that was the heart of the Roman Economic Community. The roads were straight and well kept, and for affluent Romans it became practical to commute long distances between their various holiday homes. For merchants and soldiers the distances travelled were even greater, and everywhere you went you would find towns with Roman appearances, and people speaking Greek or Latin, so that you lost any real concept of home or abroad.

In Ephesus I visited the house of a Spanish merchant – a man who had probably made a fortune out of olive oil or fish sauce – and I have seldom spent an hour in a state of such enchantment. Martin Steskal, the archaeologist, has a pleasing Austrian accent, which always adds an air of scholarship, but he behaves like an estate agent on a commission. 'I am sorry it's so dusty,' he says, and begins to lead the way through a vast series of bedrooms, bathrooms, kitchens, banqueting halls, peristyle courtyards and love chambers that recede up the hillside, the whole thing covered and protected by a vast hangar, like a terminal at Stansted.

'These were all *insulae*, expensive blocks of accommodation, and they were the property of a man called Gaius Furius Aptus. He was from Spain.'

'From Spain?' I say. 'You mean he was Spanish?'

'Oh no,' says Martin, 'he was Roman.'

Then what was he doing, I ask, owning this colossal property on the other side of the Mediterranean? This is Turkey. Why does an Andalucian build villas in Turkey?

'He made his money from agriculture, or possibly from trade,' says Martin, 'and, anyway, this was a Roman town.'

He leads the way up some stairs and under the scaffolding, to show some of the wonders of the *insula*. There is a fine mosaic of a lion, and beautifully preserved hypocausts (even on the western seaboard of Turkey it must get pretty nippy in the winter).

There are immaculate stoves, and larders, where his slaves

no doubt kept the *garum*, the olive oil and the *terra sigillata*. There is a very fine family-size latrine, where people perched on benches on three sides of a small, square room, with meditative graffiti on the walls and large keyhole-shaped apertures in the benches, and running water beneath.

Merely to have domestic water in a place like Ephesus is a sign of great wealth, and Furius Aptus obviously likes to show off. He has a lot of marble running round the wainscoting and the doorjambs. I run my fingers over the purple pattern, the frozen relic of some metamorphic geological event, and the polished rock is as cool to the touch and as redolent of looxury as it must have been to the millionaire's house guests.

Look here, I ask Martin, this stuff is in good taste, isn't it? There is nothing vulgar about it?

'Oh yes,' he assures me. 'The taste is excellent.'

Even Furius Aptus could not afford marble on every floor, and the upper storeys – destroyed by an earthquake in AD 263 – had cunningly marbled fresco paintings, on the grounds that they would only be seen by family members. The effect is not to make him seem cheapskate upstairs, but to intensify the opulence of the appointments downstairs.

Whatever one's qualms about Furius Aptus' marble obsession, he has excellent taste in paintings. There is a room of the muses, where Aptus and his chums presumably sat in sympotic revelry, and got as magnificently plastered as the walls around them. The walls are decorated with the nine muses (go on, name them: Clio, Melpomene, Erato, Terpsichore, Thalia, Polyhymnia, Euterpe, Calliope, Urania and Sappho, added on for luck, in tribute to the Lesbian lyric genius).

The painting is sketchy but elegant, and the colours are still vivid and the forms well observed. It is one of the great catastrophes of history that we have so little Greek and Roman painting. We have lost everything by the fabulous Greek Polygnotus, the Michelangelo or Raphael of his day, whose images we can only visualize through the prose descriptions of Pausanias.

But we do have some Roman painting, and as I look at the sensuously swelling abdomen of one muse, her round breasts and her neatly turned wrists and neck, I think how quickly it died, that classical insight into the human form, replaced by the weird oblongs, tapering feet, distended bellies and general childishness of medieval drawing, and how long it was before it was revived in the Renaissance.

In their sophistication, their understanding of human nature, pain and pleasure, the Romans had a civilization as exalted as anything we have seen. Martin is particularly proud of the mood and ethos of the final exhibit of the house: a fantasy, done in tiny glazed chips, on the walls and ceiling of an alcove, and representing Ariadne and Apollo. Much of it has gone, as you'd expect from bits of coloured stone stuck to the roof with 2,000-year-old glue, but there is enough to understand how beautiful the whole must have been.

There are huge globular grapes and writhing vines, and elegant if enigmatic figures. But it is the colours that are so ingenious: everything in pastel blues and greens and greys, with blobs of cadmium orange to pick up the skin tones of the god and the girl.

For a moment I want, ignobly, to suggest that it must be known as Apollo of the Serious Acne, but then feel guilty for being so trivial. As a trick of colouring it works as well as anything by Matisse or the Fauves.

This villa epitomizes the high achievements of Roman culture, and it is identical to villas across the Mediterranean and beyond. 'This villa has everything that you would find in a great house on the Palatine,' he says, meaning the Roman hill of the palaces, inhabited by Augustus and other nobs. 'The facilities are identical,' he says, waving a hand towards the kitchen.

At which point in the argument it may be that some alert readers are not satisfied. They may feel that we have so far only proved the Romanization of the elite. What about the masses? you may say. We have seen how the Romans induced a spirit of Romanitas in the local nobs, encouraged them to climb the political ladder, gave them citizenship, showed them how to make togas, gave them Virgil, instructed them in oratory, provided them with *garum*. We have seen how anyone who was anyone in Europe wanted some of that classy Roman stuff. Mmmm. Get hypocaust, get mosaic, get fountain, get on in life.

But what about the bulk of the population, in the cities and beyond? Did they feel Roman, too? How far did it permeate? It depends where you are in the empire; it depends how urbanized your province was.

But if you were anywhere in the neighbourhood of a big Roman town or city, you were invisibly sucked into the maw of a gigantic cultural processing plant. The Romans didn't just build cities across the empire. They built factories for turning barbarians into Romans.

A baffling scene of flagellation from a Pompeiian villa. When Rome fell, this understanding of the human form was to be lost for a millennium.

CHAPTER TEN

The Adventures of Lucco the Gaul

Imagine the impact of this structure on Iron Age Gauls.

Let's imagine that you are a Gaulish swineherd. You are a Gaulish swineherd called Lucco and you were born in about AD 70. You live deep in the mountainous forests of what is now the Parc National de Cévennes in the South of France, and though your life is in many ways agreeable, it cannot be called sophisticated.

You live in a hut of mud and wattles that you share with your pigs, and your domestic arrangements so perfume your skin

157

that you find it hard to get a girlfriend; not that you meet many Gaulish girls, stuck away in the hills.

When the rain comes, the hut gets wet, and you pray to Toutatis, or Belisama, or Sucellus, or Lug, or Epona, or whichever Gaulish divinity you think watches over you, and you cower in the drizzling dark with your pigs, and your personal hygiene, frankly, does not improve.

And when the sun comes out you suddenly think, stuff this for a lark. I'm pushing twenty-five. I can't sit in the forest and wait for it to happen. I'm going to walk down the valley towards those people they are always talking about, the ones with the invincible army.

I am going to find the Romans and see the world, you say, and you begin your trek. You push your way through the deep deciduous forest until you come to the River Gardon. There's no other path, so you decide to follow the bank. It's brambly and overgrown and it takes many days before the Gardon is flowing broad and slow. You are feeling pretty shattered and almost thinking of turning back, when you look at the river ahead.

At first it is so strange and frightening that you can't really take it in. It looks like an optical illusion. The whole valley ahead has been walled off, with three huge rows of bridges on top of each other, and you sink to your knees in superstitious dread.

They must be giants who did this, you think, or gods. You go closer, and you can't get over the size of it. You have barely seen a block of masonry in your life, and yet here are dressed stones far bigger than your hut. The whole thing is 49 metres high and 275 metres long.

But in spite of your very basic educational attainments and low socio-economic status, you are an enquiring kind of swineherd, and you don't just lie there grovelling. What in the name of all that is holy, you ask yourself, is this thing doing here?

You eye it squintingly, and try to work it out. It can't be just a bridge, because a bridge would not need to be 49 metres high. Why *does* it need to be so high?

Pretty soon you have worked out that it is all about the top-most tier of arches, the little ones. There must be some purpose to having them up there at that altitude. Perhaps to fire on people down below? To be able to see who is coming down the valley? Perhaps it is so high because the gods who live in it want to be near the clouds. Perhaps the idea is be able to drop rocks through the bottom of any boats in the River Gardon.

You have pretty sketchy ideas of military tactics, but none of these answers seems entirely convincing.

Just then there is a shout. A soldier has spotted you. Your first Roman!

You can see the sun glinting on his spear, and so you scuttle into the undergrowth like a rabbit. But your curiosity has been aroused. Some instinct tells you this thing must have a human explanation, and you want to find what it is. So you crawl up through the undergrowth.

You clamber up quietly, trying not to make any noise, until you come to the stone conduit at the top of the hill. You peer over the rim. Huh?

It's water. Just water, gurgling slowly southwards in a closed stone channel, all the way across the top of this extra-terrestrial structure and off into the distance. Now why would they need water, you ask yourself, when they have the River Gardon?

What you have found is the Pont du Gard, the most sensa-tional piece of municipal plumbing in history. We don't know exactly when it was built, though there are some who still think it may have been started by Augustus' right-hand man, Marcus Vipsanius Agrippa, in 14 BC.

(Agrippa was an extraordinary public servant: a first-rate general, largely responsible for the victory at Actium, he redesigned the sewers, constructed aqueducts, built the Pantheon in Rome, and commissioned a map of the empire. If Augustus had any kind of logistical or military problem his first reaction, I imagine, was to shout 'Get Agrippa!' Whether or not the Pont du Gard is his brainchild, it is on a scale that matches the energies of this Cecil Rhodes of the early Roman Empire.)

We know that the aqueduct conveyed water 32 kilometres from a spring at Uzès to the Pont du Gard, and then a further 18 kilometres on to Nîmes, 50 kilometres in all: a stupendous achievement, though only about average in length for a Roman aqueduct in Gaul. In the capital city, Lugdunum (Lyons), the water system was nourished by four aqueducts, of 25, 28, 66 and 75 kilometres respectively.

All you can see now, Lucco the Gaul, is the covered channel streaking off into the distance, forging the ravines and bursting through the scrub, and your puzzlement only increases. Where are they taking this water, and what do they want with it?

So you follow the path by the channel, giving a wide berth to any soldiers you meet, and all day long you walk through the maquis to Nîmes; and though you don't know it, you descend with the flow at an unwavering gradient of 0.4, or 25 metres in every kilometre.

You begin to pass through farmland, and again you see the hands of the Romans have reshaped nature. You pass villas, with farms attached, the villas that will turn into villages when the Dark Ages come; and though the art of Roman construction will be forgotten, and squalid wooden huts will be built in the tumbledown courtyards, the villages will survive forever on the Michelin maps of France.

You see the land is plotted and pieced into rectangular allocations for the veterans of the Roman army, and the traveller can still see these formations around Nîmes to this day.

You see vines with red and white grapes almost ready for harvest, and these are a Roman legacy far more vital and lasting than the aqueduct itself. 'Our vineyards,' says a French historian, 'are a Roman monument, one of the best-preserved Roman monuments in the country.' It is thanks to the Romans that we have Château Lafite and Mouton Cadet and other high points of civilization, though the Romans were at first grudging with the gift of Dionysus. When they introduced wine to the Gauls in the second century BC, it is said that the Gauls went wild for it. They drank it neat (a typically barbaric solecism) and they learned to love wine so much that the exchange rate was one Gaulish slave for one jar of wine.

In fact the market was so buoyant that the Romans decided to exploit it, and decreed that there should be no growing of wine or olives north of the Alps – to keep prices high. It was an example of the Italy-first policy that was to dissolve with the deepening of the Roman Economic Community.

Even in the days of the republic, Cicero spotted the selfishness of this policy. We only do it, he sniffed, '*quo plures sint nostrae vinetae nostraeque oleae*', so that our vineyards and olive groves may be more numerous. There was an instinctive feeling, in other words, that protection was alien to the Roman Common Market; and it was not long before it collapsed. (Mind you, the idea in some ways anticipates the mad control freakery of the EU's wine regime. Brussels has its own curious methods of maintaining prices – usually buying stocks into intervention storage and boiling them up into alcohol.)

Towards nightfall you come to the town of Nemausus, Nîmes, and the aqueduct runs parallel to a road. This is crowded with wagons and all sorts of things you have never seen in your life: wayside shrines to different gods, and big stone tombs, and people on horseback or being carried in litters, and though many of them are talking in Gaulish, many are jabbering away in a language you have never heard. You keep going, hand on the pommel of your Gaulish sword, still determined to solve the mystery of the weird Roman water channel.

Now the crowd is thickening as you approach the perimeter wall of Nemausus. There are vendors selling shots of wine and bits of salted cod, and biscuits coated in some pungent fish sauce, and there are girls such as you have never seen, leering at you from the flickering oil-lamp shadows and making incomprehensible suggestions. By the time you get to the huge octagonal tower constructed in the era of Augustus, for no other purpose than to show the Roman dominance of the country, you can't really take it any more. You don't want to go through the gate.

Your culture shock is complete. You slope off into the bushes outside the 6-kilometre-long Roman walls and wait for morning.

Your nightmares are interrupted. Someone is kicking you and talking loudly in Gaulish. You screw up your eyes in the sun and see that it is Uillo, a man you used to know, about ten years older than you. In fact it was about ten years ago that he disappeared from the village. Some said he'd been sold into slavery.

Now he wants to know what you are doing, and you explain about the mystery water channel, and wanting to see the Romans. Uillo laughs and offers to help.

He takes you through the gate to the place where the aqueduct debouches. It's a huge tank, with ten big tubes coming off it and running in different directions.

'Yes,' you say, 'but what's it for?'

And then Uillo explains an amazing fact about the Pont du Gard. This superhuman feat of masonry was not even strictly necessary for the survival of the people of Nîmes. There is a perfectly good spring, which supplies enough drinking water, in the town itself.

But the burghers of Nîmes wanted more water, for the fountains that played in their houses, and for their baths and for their latrines, and for washing their linen and keeping their houses clean. In other words, they wanted it mainly for luxury, and to show how Roman they had become, and in so doing they set standards for hygiene that were not to be equalled until the nineteenth century.

Now, Uillo has a job. He is a barman in a *thermopolium*, a kind of gastropub selling hot little snacks, and he offers you a bed for the night; and over the next few weeks you hang out in Nemausus, helping Uillo in the pub, and you start to understand what it means to become Roman. You walk with Uillo to his *thermopolium*, and you see the various parts of the town, and you pass through them as a piece of unadorned metal passes through the body shop and the paint shop and the assembly room of a car plant, and with each ritual process you become more Roman.

You walk down the main shopping street, a kind of porticoed mall of the sort that you can find across the known world; and you observe the grid formation in which the Romans have laid out the streets. You start to notice the ceremonies and proprieties of Roman life, the way some people are hustled out of the way to make room for others, the constant acts of propitiation before shrines or temples.

Very slowly and haltingly you start to speak some Latin, essential for understanding the orders of the legionaries who come into the *thermopolium*, and then one day Uillo says it's time for a bath. You've never had a bath before, being a swineherd; and being a Gaulish swineherd you are in need of one.

You go to the municipal baths, erected by some great man of

163

the neighbourhood, and to your amazement you are allowed in, since it is a session for shop assistants and other riffraff. You remove your matted and filthy breeches, and as you sit in the hot room and the cold room it is as if all the last traces of Gaulish mud are seeping from your pores and Romanness creeping in. In some ways it is an alarming experience, being asked to disrobe in front of all these other Gallo-Romans, and you notice a certain sniggering at your naked physical form.

'What is it?' you ask Uillo, and he produces a pair of tweezers. As you might expect from a man of the woods and glades, you have hair sprouting all over the place, and the Romans were for some reason fastidious about body hair.

From the date they conquered Britain we notice a huge increase in the archaeological incidence of tweezers, as the Britons discovered that, in Roman eyes, it was better to be a smooth man than a hairy man. So you tweezer away at your old Gaulish self, and in the most intimate way possible you are being transformed into a Gallo-Roman. You soap yourself with olive oil, you strigil off the resultant gunge, and when you go back to the changing rooms, it seems crazy to pull on those reeking old trews, and so you find a Roman tunic, of the kind Uillo wears to serve in the bar.

You leave the baths clean, shaved, tweezered, wearing a tunic and already starting to think it might be quite fine to wear one of those togas. And still the treats of the day are not exhausted.

Uillo has tickets for the games, in the amphitheatre of Nîmes, and your heart leaps: the games, the *ludi circenses*, the signature event of ancient Rome. Often on the way to the *thermopolium* you have heard the shrieking of the crowd, and you have wondered quite what went on in this vast elliptical building, which has a capacity of 21,000. You have walked past the huge double-arcade structure, and sniffed the ammoniac stench of piss and dung on sawdust, and seen the faces of the crowd as they spill out from the *vomitoria*, the rapt look of people who have been watching something both exciting and dreadful.

CHAPTER ELEVEN

The Games

Two hundred thousand people were butchered in the Colosseum alone.

The Roman games probably originated in the old Etruscan custom of slaughtering prisoners at the funerals of warriors, and the first gladiatorial combat was staged by Decimus Junius Brutus in the Roman Forum *boarium*, or cattle market, in 264 BC. Over time they became ever more elaborate and exotic and expensive, until they were not only a means of mass entertainment and control, but a terrifying statement of Roman values.

By the end of the first century AD amphitheatres were being erected all over the empire. In Rome these entertainments were the exclusive prerogative of the emperor, and in the provinces they were usually laid on by magistrates who were in some way affiliated to his cult. The provider of the games was called the *munerator*, or else, to show how little mutation there has been in the meaning of the word, the orchestrator of these depraved and titillating entertainments was known as the *editor*.

The games had three elements. There were the *venationes*, in which beasts were slaughtered in imitation of the chase, and sometimes the emperors themselves would disgrace themselves by taking part. Commodus sought to endear himself to the mob by sporting a club and a lion skin, and going around the arena butchering immobilized animals, with all the bravery of a millionaire shooting a circus rhino at a Florida dude ranch. In AD 248 the city of Rome celebrated its millennium, and on the game card that day were thirty-two elephants, a dozen tigers, more than fifty lions and six hippopotamuses. You would have thought the appetite for massacring lions becomes exhausted after a while; and you would be right. That's why they started on the poor old hippos.

The next element was the *noxii*, the execution of condemned prisoners, and here it was the Romans' idea of good solid family viewing to take a thief or murderer, saw off his feet, coat the stumps with honey and encourage the bears to eat the rest.

Although this was always gratifying to Roman taste, the outcome of an execution was never much in doubt, and it lacked the suspense of the gladiators, the climax of the games. Unlike in the movies, gladiatorial contests were normally one-on-one, and, since the fighters were expensive to train, there was a considerable financial incentive to allow the combatants to survive.

But often they didn't. They died in appalling circumstances, spilling their guts on the sand and with the cheers of the crowd in their ears. It is one of the reasons why some of us, in the end, find the Romans chilling, and hard to like, and one of the reasons so many of us prefer the Greeks. But even the Greeks came to enjoy the games, and in Ephesus archaeologists found not only the skull of a *retiarius* – the gladiator who fought with a net – they also found the three-pronged trident that had made three jagged holes at the top of his head.

Of course, there were many who disapproved. But they disapproved with all the futility of those who turn up their noses at Hollywood schlock. It was what the masses wanted; it was what kept the masses happy and it was everywhere. Every emperor had an incentive to up the ante, to find something to tickle the jaded palates of the crowd. In AD 107 Trajan laid on games in which 5,000 acts of single combat took place, which must have been as numbingly repetitive as watching someone play with a GameBoy on a plane.

Domitian had fights between gladiators and women. Commodus thought it would be jolly to get some women, and get some dwarves, and see who would be first to kill whom. It was only in 1996 that they found the amphitheatre of London. It is buried beneath the Guildhall, the place where visiting heads of state are entertained, and it has now been ingeniously restored so that you can see the very wooden runnels that were used to drain blood and ordure from the arena.

It was about the same time that they found the remains of a twenty-year-old gladiator, identifiable by some of the offerings in the grave, especially a statuette of Mercury: when the slaves came to haul the losers out of view, they were dressed as Mercury Psychopompus, the guide of the dead. But the shocking thing about this particular find was that she was a woman.

I stood there in that arena, and above my head were the

streets of the City, and the modern European urban life that is in so many ways the descendant of Rome; and yet here was something that made the Romans seem so alien as to be incomprehensible.

Modern Europe has not lost interest in seeing the slaughter of dumb animals. The Spanish bullfight is a patent descendant of the Roman habit, has the same preposterous trick of imputing 'bravery' to the poor brutes, and it takes place in buildings that are structurally identical. As for public executions, it is not so very long ago that they were one of the biggest crowd-pullers in Britain.

What does seem incredible, to our taste, is that the Romans should take so much pleasure in the slaughter of innocent people; in the death of human beings for fun. In the Colosseum alone it is estimated that 200,000 people died. What kind of sick society was it?

The gladiatorial contests were surely at the very heart of the Roman ethical system. It was a world that believed above all in winners and losers, in death and glory. There could be no glory without the risk of death, and there could be no winners without losers. Every time a gladiator died in the sand, the Romans saw the process of winning and losing acted out before them in the most violent and affecting way.

This has several psychological effects on the crowd. First and most obviously, the heroic status of the gladiators is intensified by the risks they run. Roman women became so aroused by all this manliness in the face of death that they started to behave very badly, and the old prig Augustus decreed that they should sit a minimum of six rows back from the front seats.

Juvenal tells us of Eppia, the senator's wife, who becomes so infatuated with one particular gladiator that she prefers him to children, country, sister and husband, and runs off with him to Egypt. The poet says the object of her devotion has sundry physical deformities, including scars around his face caused by the helmet, and a massive zit on his nose, but still Eppia risks everything to follow him, says Juvenal bitterly, 'because women love a swordsman'. The wife of Marcus Aurelius preferred the company of a gladiator called Martianus, which may explain the stoic resignation of the emperor's famous *Meditations*.

On the walls of the gladiator school at Pompeii we read that Celadus was '*suspirium et decus puellarum*' – the guy who made the girls sigh. In other words, gladiators were sex symbols, and in that sense Hollywood is right.

But the games had another and more important psychological function. By constantly whipping up the mob in the same waves of emotion, they created a sense of unity and identity; and by doing the same thing, in the same way, across the whole of the empire, they were an engine for cultural integration infinitely more powerful than anything we have in Europe today.

There you are, Lucco and your chum Uillo, two Gauls at various stages in the process of Romanization, and you are sitting in one of the twenty-four rows in Nîmes, looking down on this scene of unimaginable grandeur and horror.

First the statue of the emperor is paraded through the ring, to reinforce the message that this is a sacred event, a Roman event, and dedicated to the cult of Rome and its living god. Then the slaughter begins; the animal hunts; the executions; and then the killing of gladiators.

Who are they, these gladiators? They are prisoners of war, barbarians, slaves. They are losers. The matrons may find them sexy, in a pervy kind of way, but they are losers nonetheless and they are going to die at the discretion of the Roman crowd. In this sense the amphitheatres of the empire fulfil a huge symbolic role.

In every city they create a kind of internal frontier, an

171

acting out of the key elements of the Roman rise to glory: Romans standing up and cheering, barbarians dying in the dust. Everywhere you look on Roman monuments, gravestones, arches, barbarians are depicted in the same way. They are bearded, they wear trousers and they are normally rolling helplessly on the ground, skewered by the lance of some Roman horseman.

Their deaths could be tragic; they could be matters for pathetic meditation, like the deaths of the non-Roman victims in the *Aeneid*, Dido and Turnus. When we look at the statue of the Dying Gaul, made in about 200 BC, we are certainly meant to feel his pain. There he is, mullet-headed and mustachioed, with a rope collar round his neck, quietly exsanguinating through a wound in his chest.

We can feel pity for the Dying Gaul, just as the audience at the games would also have felt pity for those dying in the games. But they both make the same propaganda point. They emphasize the huge gulf between the destiny of Rome and the fate of those who were so mad as to stand in her way.

So every time you go to the games, you have that Roman sense of 'them and us'. There are Romans, all of us here in the stands, and then there are the defeated populations of the rest of the world, who supply the bleeding and the tragedy.

We have seen how Augustus used that concept of 'them and us' in his propaganda against Cleopatra, and it is that binary division of the world – into Romanitas and barbarism – that was such a powerful force for unity. But the point about these barbarians fighting in the arena was not just that they could evoke pity. They could also fight back, and fight hard and mean. One minute the recumbent barbarian could be at your feet, the next he could be at your throat; and the crowd whoops with sudden horror. In that sense the battles in the amphitheatre are like the stone battles on the triumphal arch at Orange.

They are vivid reminders of the underlying facts of the Roman Empire: that it is ringed by danger (remember Varus and the massacre in the forest), and that explains and legitimates the way the whole thing works. We need the army to preserve us from violent trousered thugs of the kind you see before you in the amphitheatre, and we need taxes to pay for the army; and the emperor to organize the whole thing.

Time and again throughout history we have seen how the peoples of a country or empire can be driven together by an external threat. The European Union was very largely the product of the Cold War, reflecting not just the desire of France and Germany to bind themselves indissolubly together, but the desire of the Europeans – sedulously encouraged by Washington – to unite against the Soviet peril.

It is no accident that the European Union has struggled a little to find a purpose since that external threat was removed. There are plenty of Europeans who think the next task should be to unite against America, but we do not need to go deeply into that argument to conclude that, whatever the external threat to modern Europe, it is nothing like as easily visualized and presented as the threat of barbarian violence; and that was symbolically enacted in the amphitheatre.

The more barbarians died in the ring, the more deeply the audience were conditioned to think of themselves as Roman.

You may have just arrived in Nîmes from the middle of some Gaulish forest, but every time you cheer in the amphitheatre you are cheering for Rome. You may speak the same language as some of these poor dolts out there, but every time you cheer you sunder yourself further from your barbarian background, and align yourself more closely with the empire and the emperor; and the Romanizing effect is all the more powerful because it takes place when you are in the grip of the most deep-seated emotions of blood lust and fear.

What pastime in modern Europe remotely approximates to the ubiquity and uniformity of the games? Bullfighting is not big in Denmark; cricket has yet to take off in Germany.

The nearest equivalent is football, and yet football loyalties are nothing like the games. Football may produce something like the same fervour, but it is the essence of football to divide nation from nation and club from club. In their obeisance to the emperor and in the moral they enacted, the games inspired loyalty to one central power.

Romanization happens by ritual and repetition, and by learning points of etiquette, like how to pass the sponge in the public latrines. The first time you go to one of these extraordinary places, with people squatting and chatting in rows, one can imagine that it is all a bit alarming. The second time you are getting the hang of it. The third time you are becoming a Roman.

And all the time you have been in Nîmes, O Lucco the Gaul, you have been doing something else that had a distinctively Romanizing effect. Every time you have been paid in your bar, every time you have bought a *garum*-flavoured snack, you have been subconsciously the object of one of the most cunning propaganda tricks of them all.

CHAPTER TWELVE

The Single Currency

Europe's original single currency. A gold coin of
Augustus from about 15–13 BC. Divi F means
Divi Filius – the Son of God.

When Jacques Delors and other European leaders decided in
the late 1980s to launch the single European currency, they
knew what they were doing. They knew that they were taking
a huge step towards a political union in much of what had
been the old Roman Empire.

It wasn't just that everyone would use the same money in
the shops, with all the advantages that would bring for trade.
They knew instinctively that it would mean taking ever more

economic decisions in common, not just about interest rates, but about tax as well.

Delors knew that the act of creating a single European currency would mean not just an economic government of Europe. In time, he hoped it would mean a political government of Europe as well.

So let us now swivel our eyes immediately back to the Roman Empire, and the lessons to be learned from the time when there really was a single currency, and one which lasted for centuries.

Let us pick up two coins, a Roman coin and a euro coin, and see the immense symbolic difference.

For most of the republican period it would be fair to say that Roman coins were a bit of a jumble. Individual aristocrats might mint them, and they would decorate them with pictures of their ancestors, or some sponsoring divinity, or perhaps a nice picture of a chariot, or the word Roma.

Until 44 BC it was unheard of in Rome for a coin to carry the image of a living human being. Julius Caesar was the first, and was assassinated almost immediately. He was followed by his adoptive son, Augustus, and for a time Augustus didn't know quite how to play it. Sometimes his head appears on the face of the coin, and sometimes he merely has some initials. Sometimes he seems to stress the old republican symbols, and sometimes he requests pictures of Capricorn, the star sign with which he was identified, or Apollo, the god who was associated with the victory at Actium.

And for quite a while he allows other Roman notables to keep striking their own coin, including a college of money-makers called the *tresviri*.

But by 11 BC all that diversity has come to an end. Augustus is the sole provider of coins in Rome, and there are some coins in which his head has spread to both sides.

There is a growing intolerance of any other iconography, even pictures of gods, unless they are specifically identified with the emperor.

There begins with Augustus a new era of Roman coinage, in which the value of the coin resides not so much in the intrinsic worth of the metal but in the authority and charisma of the image upon it. It is the head of Caesar that provides the disc with its economic validity, and from then on Roman numismatic images become increasingly persuasive in their intent.

Augustus' coinage stresses the fact of his victory at Actium, and the fact that he has brought peace, and Roman imperial currency is full of bragging such as 'Roma Aeterna' – Eternal Rome.

Who would refuse a coin that was guaranteed by such a man? How could anyone dare? To reject a coin of Caesar, the semi-divine ruler of a divine empire, would be lèse-majesté. There is even a story that under Tiberius you weren't allowed to take a coin bearing the image of Augustus into a brothel or a latrine. That may be a romantic exaggeration, but it shows the new spirit in which currency was viewed.

It was valuable because it was guaranteed by the head of the emperor. The head of the emperor stood for Rome, and the head of the emperor was found in the money bags of legionaries across the world. In Nîmes itself they minted coins in honour of Augustus, with his head on one side and a palm and crocodile on the other, in celebration of his victory over Egypt.

Now contrast the coinage of the modern euro zone. We have at least twelve different types of euro coin, some with heads, some without. The Austrians have Mozart, the Luxembourgers have a picture of Grand Duke Henri, the Irish have a harp, the Finns have a picture of some swans, the French have a tree symbolizing life, the Germans have their poor mutant eagle – and so on.

As for the banknotes, they have no national characteristics at all. The European leaders could not agree on a single person to put on their money – of course not – so they have ended up with a depressing series of schematic architectural drawings of bridges and ditches and culverts and whatnot.

My point is not that the currency is in some way devalued for being so dismal: as a store of value, there may be a merit in dullness.

It is just that the contrast with Rome is so striking: the Roman coins so clear in their political message, the euro coins so desperately fudged.

The trouble with the single European currency is that nobody really knows who is in charge of it, and therefore nobody knows in whose interest it is being run. That may present problems if there continue to be tensions between the interests of the different nations (Germany and Italy, for instance) in what is not an optimal currency zone.

Above all, the designs mean that the euro coin is of zero political and propaganda value. Whose image and super-scription is this? asks Jesus of the Roman coin. And though you would always find coins that did not have the emperor's head on them, the overwhelming likelihood in the Roman world, if you held out your palm and waited for payment, was that you would have a picture of Caesar put in your hand.

The coin was important in your life, and that underscored the importance of Caesar. Caesar was all-powerful, and that boosted the value of the coin.

What, though, if Caesar was not all-powerful? What if Caesar was defeated? What if Caesar was a bit of a buffoon?

The natural consequence of the Roman system was that if the emperor became devalued, then the coin became devalued;

and if the currency was prone to inflation, then the emperor was assumed to be a failure.

As Epictetus says, 'Whose stamp does this *sesterce* bear? Trajan's? Take it. Nero's? Chuck it out.'

We have looked so far at the system Augustus created, and the extraordinary way in which he took power and centralized it in the institution of the emperor. We have seen how that power was disseminated across the empire, and I hope I have given a persuasive account of how people became Roman and how and why they wanted to become Roman in a way that they just do not seem to want to become European. We have seen how the enormous success of that Roman system has been the inspiration for wannabes and imitators down the ages. But at the back of our minds we have had the memory of that terrible defeat of Varus at the hands of Arminius, and the knowledge that the barbarians have never really gone away. We admire Augustus for the frightening logic of his system, in which he is at the centre of an enormous web, but we know in our hearts that few of his successors will match his genius. It is time now, in the final chapter, to follow the great Edward Gibbon and to deduce the most important circumstances of the decline and fall of the Roman Empire, a revolution which will be ever remembered, and is still felt by the nations of the earth.

PART FOUR

What Went Wrong?

CHAPTER THIRTEEN

Christians, Barbarians and Barbarian Christians

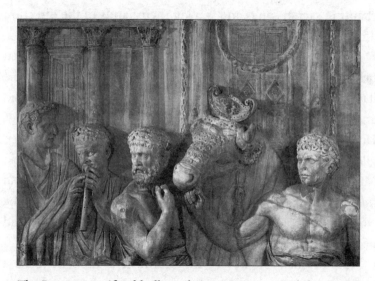

The Romans sacrificed bulls to their emperors – until the empire turned Christian.

So let us now leave our Gaulish friends Lucco and Uillo. We wave goodbye to them, quietly Romanizing in the baths or the latrines or the circus, and we wander down the crowded streets of Nîmes until we come to another astonishing sight.

It is a temple, raised high on a platform and constructed in the style typical of the Augustan epoch, with white marble and Corinthian columns and a wide flight of steps running down from the portico to the ground. These days the steps echo to the slap of the sandals of tourists, come to admire the building known as the Maison Carrée for its perfect preservation and symmetrical proportions.

It was built by our old friend Marcus Vipsanius Agrippa in about 20 BC, and 2,000 years ago the steps would have been running with blood.

In the forecourt of the temple there would have been youths and maidens with garlands and ribbons in their hair, chanting sacred songs and waving their hands in the direction of a grisly scene.

A large bull is standing patiently among a group of cowled priests, chewing his cud. He is a beautiful specimen, and he has been washed and dressed for the occasion, his curls teased and brushed as though in preparation for a fat-stock show. He is decorated with red woollen ribbons, his horns have been gilded and he has a richly decorated coverlet on his back. Muttering a prayer, the priest first sprinkles his back with *mola salsa*, the roasted wheat flour with added salt that gives us the word immolation. Then he pours a little wine on the forehead of the animal, and then he runs his knife over its back.

Now the next bit is very important. It is thought to be a good omen if the victim appears to consent to his slaughter, so the priest has a trick. Someone holds a tasty handful of feed under the beast's mouth; the bull instinctively bows his head to eat.

Tremendous! He's nodded – and tonk! – at the very moment of acquiescence the animal is stunned with a poleaxe, and then has his throat cut. Nor is that the end of the shambles.

With the help of the *haruspices* – the entrail readers – the priests roll the animal over, slit it from stem to stern, and see if the innards contain any anomalies. If everything seems more or less in order, it is assumed that the sacrifice has been accepted. And who is accepting the death of this bull? To whom are the bovine entrails dedicated?

Far away in Rome a middle-aged man is pacing up and down in his platform heels, worrying about the appalling behaviour of his daughter, Julia, the intrigues of his wife, Livia, and vaguely thinking about lunch.

They are sacrificing this bull to the emperor, but if it seems bizarre to us it seemed logical to the Romans. The ancient world was a bit like Hindu India in that divinity was all around us, and could take many forms. Indians will leave a little candle for Ganesh on one street corner, offer a prayer to Hanuman at another, and then head off for the temple of Vishnu. In the same way the Romans felt profoundly that the world was so random, and so surprising, and so frightening, that you couldn't be too careful.

They wanted the gods on their side, and, provided they were worshipped in the proper Roman fashion, it didn't matter much which gods they were. They recruited divinities from Egypt and the Middle East: Vespasian was a devotee of Isis; Elagabalus worshipped a black stone he had found in Antioch; many Romans were initiates of the cult of Magna Mater, or Cybele, whose rites climaxed in such a frenzy that the celebrants would cut their own testicles off – for what doctrinal purpose we find it hard to imagine – and still the cult was tolerated by the Romans.

In a sense, therefore, the cult of the emperor was like that of any other divinity: you didn't see him around, but he could have a big impact on your life. It wasn't so much a question of belief, as we understand it. It was a question of behaviour. Romans weren't interested in deep matters of faith, or inner spirituality: they put the emphasis on conformity and custom and practice. Provided you did right by the gods, they would do right by you; and provided you did right by the emperor and the cult of Rome, all would be well between you and the Roman Empire.

That is why there was such a boom in the Augustan cult across the Roman provinces. We have seen how in AD 19 Caius Julius Rufus was so thrilled to be made a priest of the Altar of Augustus at Lyons that he dedicated an amphitheatre, an arch and a bridge. In the museum at Mainz I saw a wonderful pillar about 13 metres high, decorated with images of twenty-eight gods, and dedicated not just to Jupiter Optimus Maximus but to Nero.

Consider the implications of this. Two new Roman citizens, Quintus Julius Priscus and Quintus Julius Auctus, both presumably of Germanic origin, are so delighted with their status and with all the money they have made from the Roman soldiers that they have paid for a huge monument to the health of one of the biggest creeps in history, a man who killed his mother, punched his pregnant wife so hard in the stomach that she miscarried and died, and castrated his favourite slave so that he could marry him/her. But he was a god; he incarnated the idea of Rome, and it was important to show him respect.

No less than the games, the theatre, the baths and everything else, the cult of the emperor bound everything together. It was the egg white in the great diverse pudding of Rome, and if we switch our eyes now to modern Europe we can see what a yawning gap there is in our own culture.

Where are the Euro-rituals? Where is the Euro-religion? Whereare the symbols around which the people of the continent could possibly unite?

It was the great Jacques Delors, the former President of the Commission, and an ardent Catholic, who saw this lacuna;

and I well remember the despairing efforts of a priest in one of his think-tanks, who was asked to create a 'spiritual dimension' for the Community. He was on the right track, of course, but the task was hopeless.

Remember those happy wheezes in the Euro-constitution: that there should be a European national anthem (Beethoven's Ninth), and a Europe day (the birthday of former French foreign minister Robert Schumann on 9 May), on which all the peoples of Europe should bunk off and feel European. They were junked when the French and the Dutch threw out the constitution; but even if they are one day adopted they are nothing next to the universal potency of the imperial cult. Across the empire the populations were watching priests sacrifice to the same emperor, in the same way, and they even had the image of the head of Augustus stencilled onto their cowls.

And because it was of such huge political importance, and because it was so essential for the unity of the empire, the cult of the emperor could not be ignored. You could worship what other gods you chose, but you had to make obeisance to the emperor and to Rome.

That was why the Romans so disliked the Christians, and to a lesser extent the Jews. They were both monotheists, and they both refused to worship any other god. So when things went wrong, as they always did, it was very easy for the ancient pagan mind to blame those who refused to accept the proper religion of the community, and who had thereby made the gods angry.

The Jews at least had the merit of antiquity: their Yahweh was very old, and the Romans respected things that had been done in a particular way for a very long time. But the Christians! There was nothing time-hallowed in their refusal to honour the emperor. It was just insulting. So they called the

Christians 'atheists' and 'haters of the human race'. The pagans wilfully misunderstood the doctrines of the sacrament and brotherly love, and accused Christians of cannibalism and incest.

From the time of Nero onwards the Christians were liable to persecution. When things were going badly there would be pogroms, and the Christians would be set on fire or fed to the beasts, like the forty-eight who were martyred in Lyons in AD 177, in the amphitheatre built by Caius Julius Rufus.

See here, said one North African governor to some Christian would-be martyrs: we don't want to kill you, we just want you to do the very minimal thing of showing some allegiance to the imperial cult. Is that really too much?

It was. The Romans were amazed by the eagerness with which some of the early Christians sought martyrdom. Members of the hard-line Donatist sect would actually stand on street corners and ask passers-by to cut their throats. In their suicidal behaviour, in their belief in an afterlife, and in their rejection of the values of the culture in which they found themselves, the early Christians evoke obvious comparisons with Islamic suicide bombers of today.

In both cases we have on the one hand a big, broad, syncretic religion and a slightly decadent society obsessed with fame and pleasure; and on the other hand we have a group of zealots whose religious rejectionism involves a logical refusal to accept the authority of the state in which they find themselves.

The Christians were eventually to triumph, and the reason for this triumph is one of the great questions of world history. There are those who say that Christianity was doomed to succeed because it was and is 'true', but I hope, without ruling that out, that we are entitled to consider other possibilities as well.

We have seen that Rome was a society based on glory and triumpha, and show, and ceaseless competition between macho males. This is all very well as long as things are going well for Rome, and for the males in question. But what about the women, and the slaves, and the downtrodden? What about the losers? And what about when things don't go well for Rome?

It should not be too obvious to state that Christianity offered an alternative ethic, in which the disappointments and disasters of the world could be assuaged in heaven. The losers – the meek – would be rewarded; and that was attractive, especially if you were in a position of enforced meekness.

Christianity also had the advantage of simplicity. The pagan religion flourished to the end, but it may be that the sheer cosmopolitanism of the Roman world was inimical to polytheism. It was easier to be cynical about the divinities of your city-state when you travelled around and met so many others. And the beauty of the Roman Empire, from the point of view of the Christian evangelist, was, of course, that you could spread the new gospel as quickly and penetratingly as fish sauce.

The greater the problems of the empire, the better Christianity did; and it is easy to see why people should be increasingly sceptical about the claims of the imperial cult, and more and more willing to listen to a new theology. In the third century Rome entered a period of political and economic crisis, in which inflation of the currency was matched by a collapse of the status of the emperor and the whole imperial class.

As with many mature societies, the population of the empire was not rising as fast as before; and yet multitudes were increasingly to be found on the borders, tribes from northern and central Europe, displaced by heaven knows what events in the east. The more trouble there was on the borders, the bigger the demands on the army. It doubled in size, to 600,000 – and yet the troops had to be paid from the same tax base.

The result was inflation. In the mid-first century AD, the silver content of the sestertius was 97 per cent. By AD 250 it has fallen to 40 per cent and by AD 270 it was only 4 per cent. That charismatic Roman coin was devalued, and so, therefore, was the man whose image and superscription had once been intrinsic to that value – the emperor.

When Augustus invented the job, he had gone through an elaborate routine of rejecting honours and pretending to be an ordinary citizen. In reality his power was supreme. His decision to turn down his eighth consulship and 'restore the republic' was just the bogus self-deprecation of a man who is the unchallenged ruler of the world, and who is acknowledged as such in men's hearts. With the facts of authority in his grasp, who needed the trappings?

As time went on, the heirs of Augustus found it ever more difficult to live up to his example. Augustus died at the vast age of seventy-five, in the arms of his wife, having determined his succession and organized an empire that was to last for centuries. But in the second half of the third century, imperial authority was contested between dozens of soldier-emperors and pretenders, many of them meeting ludicrous and embarrassing ends.

In AD 260 the emperor Valerian was captured by the Persian king Shapur I and spent the rest of his life acting as the footstool of the Great King, getting down on all fours whenever he wanted to mount his horse. In the end the Persian took pity on his captive, killed him, flayed him and used the skin as a wall-hanging. It is hard to imagine that this kind of thing added greatly to the reverence of the cult of the emperor.

The crisis demanded a radical solution, and in AD 293

Diocletian instituted the 'tetrarchy', or rule by four, in which the empire was divided into two 'Augusti', assisted by two 'Caesars'. Rome was no longer the administrative capital of the empire, and with the four co-gerents constantly on the move, stability was restored – at a price.

Damage had been done to the central unifying concept of the Roman emperor; and so, unlike Augustus, Diocletian and his successors began to insist that they be treated with more than customary reverence. When Augustus was emperor, he was so relaxed about his own personal security that one of his friends had himself carried into his presence in a litter – from which he sprang armed with a knife, simply to show the emperor what risks he was running.

By the beginning of the second century we are told that people approach the emperor Trajan '*religiose*' – with religious awe. By the time of the Antonines in the middle of the second century, the presence of the emperor is protected by all sorts of doorkeepers and *silentiarii* (whose job it was to call for a bit of 'ush for the emperor). Diocletian goes that final step, and demands that people crawl into his presence on all fours, in what the Greeks called *proskynesis*.

Such were the desperate steps he took to restore the authority of the emperor; and in the same spirit he resorted to pure lunacy to restore the value of the currency. Showing a degree of economic illiteracy that he shared with the Heath government of the 1970s, he instituted price controls in 301, posting up a vast list of price maxima, and threatening shopkeepers with execution if they asked more than a certain amount for a pound of liver or a schooner of oil.

It was a disaster, of course. The traders refused to sell at the prices demanded by the emperor, kept their goods off the market – and prices went yet higher. All the time the number of bureaucrats was rising, to enforce such pieces of madness. By the fourth century the number of officials had swollen from around 150 senior people, running the whole empire, to at least 30,000. Ambitious parents would put down the names of their children at birth, so that they could become bureaucrats, and the more bureaucrats there were the less tax came in, because one of the advantages of being a bureaucrat was that you didn't have to pay tax. By AD 400 there were 6,000 jobs in Rome that commanded senatorial status.

For the first time Rome was afflicted by the sclerosis that we have seen in so many modern European economies, when the bureaucracy becomes so big that its prime concern becomes self-perpetuation.

And almost every time Rome was in crisis, or the emperor was in trouble, the response was to turn on the enemies within – the Christians, the people who had the wrong set of beliefs, and who must surely be the cause of the trouble. In 250 the emperor Decius decreed that everyone would have to perform an act of worship of the emperor; and to smoke out the recusant Christians, he issued the worshipper with a ticket on completion of their duties. If an individual failed to produce a ticket, the obvious conclusion was that he was a Christian, and worthy of persecution. In 303, just after the price controls disaster, Diocletian gave the Christians another terrible mauling.

So it might have gone on, had it not been for the decision of one man, who made a personal declaration of faith that was to change the world. There is still great controversy as to his motives. Did he really see a cross in the sky, before the battle of the Milvian Bridge in 312? Was there really a celestial scribble reading '*in hoc signo vinces*'? 'You will conquer in this sign.' Or was it '*en touto nika*', in Greek? Perhaps it was in both, like the subtitles of a Belgian film.

Some people say that Constantine was just doing the smart

thing, and going with the tide of conversion; others that Christianity was not yet that widespread, and that this was a genuine leap of faith. Whatever his reasons, when Constantine became a Christian in 312 he transformed the ideological basis of the Roman Empire. By switching to monotheism, and discounting all other divinities, he made a lasting change to the theological position of the emperor.

In many ways the change was very far from obvious. Constantine still occupied the supreme human position; he was still the figurehead of the new religion; he was still exalted; he was still depicted in pieces of sculpture, though far bigger than anything Augustus had commissioned for himself. He was the object of quite hysterical flattery and veneration. He was going to take this new state religion and use it to bring fresh glory and honour to Rome.

But there was one critical theoretical distinction that was to become more important over time.

The worship of the emperor Augustus was in itself a political act, an act of loyalty to Rome. The act of Christian worship did not necessarily carry any such political implications.

When the destroyers of Rome were to come, many of them were barbarians who had already converted to Christianity. In a profound but almost invisible way, the coming of Christianity changed the assumptions on which the empire was based. All emperor worshippers were loyal to Rome; not all Christians were loyal to the emperor.

It was the beginning of the end of the magical web that Augustus created – the semi-religious identification between the citizen and the central power. It was the beginning of the end of the egg white in the cake.

As a coagulating ingredient, Europe has never found anything to match it.

* * *

There were other important and more visible ways in which Christianity began to transform what it meant to be a Roman. Already at the beginning of the third century AD – 206 – the Christian writer Tertullian was attacking the games and the theatre. Women should be strictly veiled, and all the ornaments and finery of the pagans were to be deprecated. The baths, needless to say, were immodest.

But it was only after the conversion of Constantine that the movement against pagan culture got into full swing, and it did not take long for the reaction to become ferocious. In 391 the last emperor of a united empire, Theodosius I, made a speech in which he outlawed blood sacrifice – no more cattle would be slaughtered to anyone, let alone the emperor. He even attacked the habit of looking at the beauties of classical sculpture, saying, 'no one is to go to the sanctuaries, walk through the temples, or raise his eyes to statues created by the labour of man'.

In the same year this zealot extinguished the eternal flame in the Temple of Vesta, and told the Vestal Virgins that their virginity was no longer demanded by the state. In 393 he cancelled the last Olympic games of antiquity, on the grounds that they were decadent, corrupt and involved a good deal of semi-nudity.

By now bands of aggressive Christian monks were pulling down the pagan temples, and among the wonders lost to the world was the Serapeum, the temple of Serapis, in Alexandria, destroyed on the orders of Theodosius.

In this new climate it is no surprise that the Roman ruling classes seemed to lose their old euergetic zeal. They stopped building those fabulous creations – done with private money and for the public good – the temples, baths, theatres, malls, latrines and amphitheatres of Europe.

Rich people gave their money to churches, and though the

churches undoubtedly spent the money on worthy causes, such as helping the poor, there is not much left to see. Suddenly there was a new ideal of behaviour: the ascetic, the man who rejected books – even burned them – and sought contemplation in the desert. For a society whose heart was in urban civilization, and the joy of adorning the cities, it was a profound change of orientation.

The citizens of the early Roman Empire would have thought it not just silly, but also shamefully selfish, to climb on top of a pillar and meditate. The Christians thought it saintly.

It is not fashionable these days to cite Edward Gibbon, but I cannot help feeling there is a grain of truth in the following mordant analysis:

> The clergy successfully preached the doctrines of patience and pusillanimity; the active virtues of society were discouraged, and the last remains of the military spirit were buried in the cloister; a large portion of public and private wealth was consecrated to the specious demands of charity and devotion; and the soldiers' pay was lavished on the useless multitudes of both sexes, who could only plead the merits of abstinence and charity.

Now the Gibbonian view, as you can see, is that the Roman Empire was morally sapped by Christianity, and that made it vulnerable to the barbarians. All that meekness, he argues, all that turning the other cheek: no wonder the Romans lost. In recent times he has had some support from the great A. H. M. Jones, who agrees that quite a lot of military and administrative talent was probably diverted into the church.

I have a sneaking sympathy for the old Gibbonian analysis; but the closer we look at what really happened, the clearer it is that the real cause of the fall of Rome was not inside the empire, but outside it.

The Roman Empire was not, like so many of its successors, torn apart by uprisings among its subjugated races – far from it. It is, of course, true that there were undercurrents of dissatisfaction, dislike of taxation, and what we in this book have called Romano-scepticism.

There were the revolts in Gaul in AD 21 under Florus and Sacrovir; and though the causes were complex there is certainly more than a dash of Gaulish national feeling. There was the revolt of Boudicca and the Iceni in AD 62, in which the causes unquestionably included feelings of national outrage at the Roman treatment of their royal family. It is surely legitimate to think that when Tacitus gives Calgacus his angry and passionate defence of British freedom, he is articulating sentiments that genuinely existed.

In spite of the Moulinex effect of the empire, we have evidence of good old national prejudice, and not just Juvenal the satirist raging hyperbolically against foreigners such as Greeks or Syrians.

There is a lovely tablet from Vindolanda on Hadrian's Wall in which a group of Belgian soldiers speaks disparaginglyof the *Britunculi* – little Britons. That's right: Brits being disparaged by Belgies.

These are the proto-national sentiments that were inspired by the Roman invasions, and then occluded during the long period of the *Pax Romana*.

In these grunts and scratchings we can detect the disparate cultures that pre-existed the incoming tide of Romanization. When that tide went out, and the empire fell, it was to leave rock pools of Roman water, separate ecosystems that were to produce the various languages and cultures of Europe today.

But when the empire fell, it wasn't the resentful tribes inside the empire that were the problem; they had largely become Roman.

What did for Rome were the waves of Vandals, Alans, Franks, Alamanni, Goths, Huns, Tervingi and Greuthingi, and what they wanted, of course, was not to destroy Rome. Like everyone else, they wanted to become Roman, and the story of the fall of the Roman Empire is a long and complex tale of how the Romans completely failed to manage that desire.

Huge invasions of Goths crossed the Rhine in AD 406, and one sultry afternoon in 410 an army led by the Arian Christian Alaric entered Rome by the Via Salaria, a road near the station that is now full of prostitutes, and sacked the city. In 476 the last emperor, Romulus Augustulus, was deposed from Ravenna. These events have come down to us as cataclysms; and they were. It is just that they didn't necessarily feel like that to the Romans at the time.

You can be taking an active part in your own decline and fall and not be aware what it is going on.

When they found they couldn't beat them, they let them in. They let them have their own huge territories, first in Thrace and then in Gaul, and slowly they started to lose sight of that distinction that had made the empire so cohesive. The empire started to lose that vital sense of 'them and us'.

After a while, it was hard to tell who was a barbarian and who was a Roman. There were Romans with moustaches, and there were barbarian generals who seized the imperial throne. The whole of Italy was run by the Ostrogoths, and Spain was run by the Vandals.

They weren't proper Romans. They had a vague idea how everything worked, and they did their best, but the overall effect was a bit like a gigantic chimpanzees' tea party.

* * *

197

In the end, Rome fell. It was not a 'transformation'. It was not an 'evolution'. It was not the mere replacement of one culture by another. It was a political, economic and cultural disaster on an unparalleled scale, and quite without any compensations.

The army disintegrated. The population shrank. Plagues raged. In Britain the skill of making pottery was lost for 300 years. In France men forgot how to make roof tiles, and all over Europe the post-holes of pathetic huts were dug in the mosaics of magnificent villas. Cattle had been 115.5 centimetres at the withers in the Iron Age, and in the empire had grown to 120 centimetres. Now in the early medieval period they shrank back to 112 centimetres.

Above all, it was the end of the amazing literacy of the Roman world. Bryan Ward-Perkins, of Trinity College, Oxford, has pointed correctly to the graffiti from the brothel of Pompeii as evidence of the informal and everyday manner in which Romans used the written word to celebrate innocent pleasures that were to become the subjects of Christian guilt and hysteria. It was not just Virgil who was buried in the night of the Dark Ages; it was reading and writing.

It is the very sharpness and savagery of that transition that intensifies the sense of loss. The memory of Rome, the dream of Rome, is all the sweeter for the appalling contrast with what followed.

That is why people have for so long gazed back at Rome, through the wastes of the Dark Ages, and tried to recover the best of that happy epoch of the *Pax Romana*.

If we in modern Europe were to take the best of ancient Rome, and leave the worst, what would we take, and what would we leave?

We would avoid the slavery and the mines and the psychotic cult of the ego; the militarism and the cruelty. But we would want the religious tolerance, the racial tolerance, the intellectual tolerance and curiosity. We would surely want the laissez-faire government of the High Empire, in which the economy grew and people prospered with minimal bureaucracy and regulation.

If the Romans are to be any guide, we would surely welcome the Turks; not just on grounds of religious tolerance, but also because Turkey, after all, was where the empire survived for another 1,000 years until 1453. It would be good to bring the Turks in, and reunite the two halves of the Roman Empire.

It would be good to recapture that enormous public-spirited creative energy of the Romans, to say nothing of the efficiency that allowed them to rule an empire of 80 million with 150 officials.

One thing we in Europe must perhaps accept is that we will never recover that vast Roman sense of political unity, with the face of every citizen turned like a sunflower towards the political centre. That was pre-eminently the achievement of Augustus, and it seems very unlikely to be repeated.

To do so would involve the creation of an emperor, with semi-divine status, having a direct relationship with every citizen in his divinely ordained empire.

No, we will never reproduce the Roman Empire, with its huge and peaceable unity of races and nations. But if history teaches us anything it is that we are fated never to stop trying.

ACKNOWLEDGEMENTS

It may seem eccentric to begin by thanking a Labour cabinet minister, but I owe a debt to Charles Clarke for the candour with which he spoke in 2003 when he was Secretary of State for Education. He was discussing the study of ancient languages, literature and history, and offered the opinion – quite unprompted – that 'education for its own sake' was 'a bit dodgy.' He went on to say that he would 'not be much occupied' if the study of classics were to die out altogether in Britain. A few weeks later the British state's chief custodian of scholarship and learning made a speech in which he said that the study of medieval history was merely 'ornamental' and did not deserve taxpayers' money.

As soon as I read those words, I was filled not just with fury, but also with real terror that these could be the instincts of people with the power of life and death over the academic curriculum. And I was grateful to Clarke for showing so clearly why you can never really trust other people to run the country, and why it is important, if you care about something, to seek political office and to try to wrest control from the hands of the thugs and barbarians.

As it happens, the student body of Britain responded magnificently to Charles Clarke. They decided that if a New Labour minister was going to denounce classics as 'a bit dodgy', there was plainly much to commend the discipline. Since then there has been a small boom in classical studies; and it is my belief that this country would lose nothing if that boomlet were to turn into a wholesale revival, and classics were studied systematically not just in some of the more exclusive higher education establishments, but in much larger numbers of maintained-sector secondary schools as well.

I say this partly because of the argument advanced in this book: that the ancient world is not just the creator of the modern world. It still has a huge amount to teach us; and I hope that in this discussion of how the Romans created a single political culture and sense of identity in Europe, I have cast an interesting sidelight on one of the most important and most intractable questions of our times.

Of course classics passes the Charles Clarke test of utility, and with flying colours. It is far more vocationally useful than 'media studies', for instance, which has expanded by 464 per cent over the last ten years. It is no disrespect to students or teachers of that subject to say that many of its adherents would be far better off reading classics full-time, and reading the newspapers in their spare time ...

But I don't want to play Charles Clarke's game. I refuse to submit to his dreary utilitarian calculus. I would not mind if he could prove that classics added not a penny to Britain's GDP. It is still worth studying as an end in itself.

The civilizations of the Greeks and Romans made our language, made our art, our architecture, our political institutions, our literature. They made us.

If this book encourages a single person to want to study this stuff, then my mission will have been accomplished.

I would like to thank all the people who helped to produce this book and the BBC TV series, a star-studded cast of academics and experts across Europe.

Over the past year they have helped fill my head with a vast quantity of Roman rubble, and in so far as I have been able to turn it into some kind of a mosaic, it is entirely thanks to them. It goes without saying that responsibility for all errors is mine and mine alone.

In no particular order, they are: Dr Sander Evers, Assistant Professor, University College, Utrecht; Professor Paolo Cesaretti, Professor of Byzantine Studies, University of Chieti; Antonio Martino, Italian Defence Minister; Dr Andrea Carandini, Professor of Archaeology, La Sapienza, University of Rome; Professor Elio Lo Cascio, Professor of Roman History, University of Naples; Jacques Lasfargues, Conservator and Director of the Archaeology of the Rhone; Nicolas Duntz, disgruntled French farmer; Guy Bastianelli, cheesemaker; Professor Karl-Joachim Holkeskamp, Professor of Ancient History, University of Cologne; Professor Egon Schallmayer, Director, Saalburg Fort Museum; Dr Michael Klein, Head of Archaeology, Mainz; Dr Martin Steskal, Austrian Archaeological Institute, Vienna; Dr Hans-Joachim Kann, Director of Study, University of Trier; Professor Kai Brodersen, Professor of Ancient History, University of Mannheim; Professor Charlotte Roueche, Head of Department, Byzantine and Modern Greek Studies, King's College London; Professor Norman Stone, Professor of International Relations, University of Bilkent; Professor Ilber Ortayli, Director, Topkapi Palace; Nefise Bazolglu and Melek Taylan, representatives of the intelligentsia of Istanbul.

All of these people gave generously of their time, but some of the dons were especially heroic in their efforts to instruct me. Professor Paolo Cesaretti, Professor of Byzantine Studies, Chieti, introduced me to the concept of female gladiators; Jeremy Paterson, Senior Lecturer in Ancient History, University of Newcastle-Upon-Tyne, drew attention to the parallels between ancient and modern religious fundamentalist martyrdom.

Professor Greg Woolf, of St Andrews University, showed me around the latrines, baths and shopping malls of ancient Vaison, and joined me in acting out a sacrifice to the imperial cult (I was the bull; no animals were harmed). I am deeply indebted to him, as I am to Professor Andrew Wallace Hadrill, Director of the British School in Rome, who explained so much about Augustus.

Dr Benet Salway saved me from some errors, but above all I should thank the academics who have read the book in draft, Matthew Nicholls of Queen's College, Oxford, who showed me the necklace of the twelve Caesars – which may be the distant inspiration of the Euro flag; Dr Lisa Bligh of St Hilda's, Oxford, and especially her husband, Ed Bispham, of Brasenose, a wise and prodigiously knowledgeable academic who showed me Monte Testaccio and defended my theories against the scepticism of some other academics.

The best next step for anyone who has got this far in this book is to look these people up on the web, and invest heavily in their publications.

I would never have had the joy of these conversations, of course, had it not been for Tiger Aspect Productions and the BBC. My first debt is to Tom Webber, who cooked it all up, and then to all the TV supremos who made it such a pleasure to track the Romans around Europe: Frank Hanly, the director, a monument of patience and kindliness; Colin Case, the cameraman, and John Pritchard the sound man, both of whom tended to get to the heart of the matter pretty incisively; Carla de Nicola, who provided the pink shirts, Jenny Evans, Toby Follett, David Irvine, Martin Cooper and Riaz Meer. I should also express my heartfelt thanks to Charles Brand, top man at Tiger Aspect, Lucy Hetherington of the BBC, and finally those without whom it would not have been possible to write this book: everyone at the *Spectator*, notably Stuart Reid,

Ann Sindall, Rudi the sandwich man and Mary Wakefield, who put up with my absences really rather well; my agent, Natasha Fairweather; my publisher, Susan Watt; my wife, Marina; and extra special number one thanks to the director and producer David Jeffcock, a Regius professor manqué, whose head is so stuffed with scholarship about Rome that he really should have written the book himself.

LIST OF ILLUSTRATIONS

Page